THE COMPLETE GUIDE TO
MARYLAND
HISTORIC MARKERS

Written by
JOE A. SWISHER

Photography by
ROGER MILLER

Roger Miller

Joe Swisher

IMAGE PUBLISHING, LTD.

IMAGE PUBLISHING, LTD.
1411 Hollins Street/Union Square

410-566-1222   Baltimore, Maryland 21223   FAX 410-233-1241

DEDICATION

I would like to dedicate this book to my family **SUE, SUSAN,** and **ELIZABETH** for their love and support.

Joe Swisher, Author
9-3-96

DEDICATION

I would like to dedicate this book to the memory of **MINNIE HERSCHER SCHOEN** and **WILLIAM ANTHONY SCHOEN,** who I always knew as Grandma and Grandpa. Your wisdom, joy and love is still with us all.

Roger Miller, Photographer
9-3-96

SPECIAL THANKS

We would like to thank everyone who had a part in the success of this book. We would especially like to thank the following:

We would like to thank all the people and organizations who took the time and effort to preserve and promote the history of our state by erecting these historic markers.

We would like to thank **Governor Parris Glendening** for writing the foreword to this book.

We would like to thank **AMY MAYO** for typing the Draft Text.

We would like to thank **MARY LOUISE DE SARRAN,** of the Maryland Historical Trust, for her help in researching the files.

Joe A. Swisher and Roger Miller

CREDITS

Research by Joe A. Swisher
Text by Joe A. Swisher
Photography by Roger Miller
Design by David Miller and Roger Miller
Editing by Roger Miller
Typesetting and Layouts by Delta Graphics & Communications, Inc.
Printed in Hong Kong

INFORMATION

ISBN # 0-911897-26-7 (1st edition)

Library of Congress Catalog Number 96-078519

ORDERS

For direct orders call or write for specific cost and postage and handling to the above address. Discounts available for stores, institutions and corporations. Minimum orders are required.

FT. McHENRY - Standing guard at the entrance of the Baltimore Harbor is Ft. McHenry. On September 13, 1814 the fort withstood a bombardment of the British fleet and saved both Baltimore and our Nation. Francis Scott Key, inspired to see our flag standing that next morning, wrote the lines of a poem that became our National Anthem. (See page 38, marker 16, and page 125 , marker 9).

U.S. NAVAL ACADEMY, NOON FORMATION - In 1845 Annapolis became the home of the U.S. Naval Academy. The Midshipmen line up before every noon meal in front of Bancroft Hall which is named for, the Secretary of the Navy and founder of the Naval Academy, George Bancroft.

TABLE OF CONTENTS

Ft. Frederick, Washington County

Image Publishing, Ltd., Joe Swisher and Roger Miller would like to
acknowledge and thank the following for their support in publishing this book.
Their assistance will allow everyone to appreciate the richness of Maryland history.

• **State of Maryland**

and

• **Guardian Transportation, Inc.**

• **Taylor Technologies, Inc.**

• **Legg Mason Wood Walker, Inc.,
Bel Air, Maryland Branch**

• **MCA Research Corporation**

• **Elkridge Furnace Inn**

• **Maryland Film Office**

• **Scheer Partner's, Inc.**

• **Philips Technologies**

FOREWORD
By Governor Parris N. Glendening

As Governor, I have had the pleasure to travel extensively across our beautiful historic state. No matter how often I visit the rolling hills and mountains of Western Maryland and the pastoral waterfront villages of the Eastern Shore, or enjoy the enriching cultural opportunities available in the Baltimore and Washington metropolitan centers, I am constantly amazed and proud about how much Maryland has to offer to our people, newcomers and visitors. With Maryland's many scenic wonders and rich cultural diversity, we are truly worthy of the distinction of being "America in Miniature."

In order to capture the unique spirit of Maryland, it is important to learn about the historic people, places and events that shaped our state's character and continue to impact our daily lives. In *The Complete Guide to Maryland Historic Markers,* devoted history buffs, vacationing families and interested citizens will find an invaluable resource in locating these landmarks and developing an understanding of their local and national significance. Comprehensive yet easy to follow, this collaboration by Joe Swisher and Roger Miller takes the reader on a riveting journey through the generations. It takes us to St. Mary's City, where Maryland's first European settlers sought religious freedom and planted the seeds of tolerance.

Those who wish to remember America's revolutionary spirit can traverse the "General's Highway", the route taken in 1783 by General George Washington through Cecil, Harford, and Anne Arundel Counties to our current State House, where he resigned his commission in the Continental Army. Civil War scholars will be drawn to Edwards Ferry in Montgomery County and may walk the hallowed battlefields of Antietam in Washington County and Monacacy in Frederick County. Finally, those with a passion for colonial and early American architecture can plan their next vacation around visits to Baltimore City's Mount Clare Mansion, the Hammond-Harwood House of Annapolis, or Dorchester County's Trinity Episcopal Church, which is America's oldest church still in active use.

Today, Maryland is poised at the threshold of new greatness. Once reliant largely upon heavy manufacturing, it is now emerging as a global leader in the development and marketing of information technology and health services. We have invested record resources on behalf of our public schools, and are still setting new standards for accountability and academic achievement. At the same time, we are making a concerted effort with local governments and the private sector to revitalize the neighborhoods of our youth.

Along the way, we have all benefited greatly from the lessons of our storied past. Only by drawing from the experiences of Charles Carroll, Enoch Pratt, Harriet Tubman and others will our children fulfill their unlimited potential. This book is a most educational and enjoyable place to start. Best wishes for an unforgettable journey through time and across the great State of Maryland!

Parris N. Glendening

MARYLAND STATE HOUSE - is the oldest state house still in legislative use in the country. On December 23, 1783 General George Washington resigned his commission before the Continental Congress in the room pictured above. (See page 15, marker 1 and page 17, marker 19).

PREFACE

I have always been interested in roadside historical markers as I have traveled around Maryland. Quite often it seemed like I passed them before I could read them. For a long while I did not take the time to backtrack to see what they said or look around to see what they were describing. As I became more aware of the history of Maryland and had the time, I began to stop and read these markers and investigate the sites they represented. The more I investigated, the more I began to wonder how many markers were in the state, what were their themes and how did the state determine a marker was needed. My questions on the markers kept mounting and I searched for a publication that might describe them. None was available. In fact the more research I did, the more aware I became that there was a need for a source documenting the program to date.

This book is intended to document what I have learned about the program, provide a guide to all known markers, and possibly revive an interest in the Maryland Roadside Historical Marker Program. Hopefully this book will allow you to enjoy and understand the history of Maryland as presented in these markers.

JOE A. SWISHER, AUTHOR

I have searched for and located most of these historic markers over the years trying to find different sites around the state. I have pulled up in front of them in a cloud of dust with a "semi" on my tail. I have stopped state and local police to enquire where the site described was located. I have traversed fields and forged streams searching for a particular site. I have done this in every county of the state and in Baltimore City. Most of the time I found what I was looking for and sometimes considerably more.

I assumed that these historical markers were set down, by "divine historic intervention", to guide lost photographers to all the right places in Maryland. In other words, I never really had a clue to how these markers got to where they were. When Joe Swisher presented this idea to me, my response was, " Yes! Of course someone had to be responsible for these markers." This is a great story of private and public cooperation to document Maryland's history. Taken as a whole, a great "picture" of Maryland's past is presented in his compilation of these markers. The result is this book which I hope you will read, use, and enjoy.

ROGER MILLER, PHOTOGRAPHER

FT. McHENRY - This is a reenactment of the firing of a canon used in the War of 1812. Period reenactments take place at the fort regularly, mostly on the weekends. The giant flag that flew over the fort during the War of 1812 was made by Mary Pickergill, whose home on East Pratt Street in Baltimore, is now a national shrine known as "The Flag House".

INTRODUCTION

Maryland has an important place in the birth of our nation. There is no one book you can read that would provide the total history of this great state. The history of this state could be thought of as a series of individual events that when taken together create a historical mosaic of what we are. This book contains over 700 historic stories that are important pieces of this mosaic. These stories were considered by the citizens of Maryland to be important enough to be preserved as historical markers along the roads of our state.

BACKGROUND - HISTORY

Maryland roadside historical markers are concise stories about people, places and/ or events that have been deemed by interested groups as noteworthy of our heritage. The first statewide effort to erect the historical texts occurred in 1932 with a series of markers commemorating the bicentennial of George Washington's birth. Two years later the State Roads Commission erected 90 markers across the state. The placement of those markers coincided with the expansion of the highway system and the birth of the fledgling tourism industry brought on by the increased use of the automobile.

Early on the Maryland Historical Society helped to coordinate the project and has played a fundamental role in the marker program ever since. It assumed the management of the entire program in the 1970's. During this period, the program operated on a volunteer basis with the applicant responsible for the historical documentation and funding.

Recognizing the need to reestablish public support for the program, legislation was enacted in 1985 establishing state sponsorship for the roadside historical marker program. On June 1, 1988, responsibility was transferred to the Maryland Historical Trust. This state agency is charged with taking the lead in identifying, evaluating, and protecting Maryland's historical and cultural resources.

In most respects, the program remains unchanged. The traditional silver and black metal markers have been retained and the Maryland Historical Society continues to assist with the evaluation of the marker proposals. The most important change is the introduction of limited public funding to supplement the highly successful private efforts. Private funding is still required for sites of local significance. State funds are made available, on a competitive basis, to assist with the erection of markers commemorating people, events, and places of special significance to the entire state.

Since the beginning of the program in the 1930's, the State Roads Commission, the Maryland Historical Society, and the Maryland Historical Trust have erected over 700 markers, of which approximately 600 are still standing across the State. Being highway markers, there has been some attrition due to wrecks, road changes, vandalism, budget cuts, and probably just carelessness. Some early markers have been replaced by more accurate texts. I also know that some historical markers have been removed because the homes being described were still in private ownership. The public did not know this or respect the privacy of the owners. However, this book attempts to document all historical markers whether they are still standing or not. We believe all the stories are part of the historical "picture" we are attempting to document.

SPONSORSHIP

One area that the research on the marker program turned up that was particularly interesting was the private organizations and/or state agencies that sponsored these markers. Of the approximate 700 roadside markers that have been developed, over 150 sponsors or combination of sponsors have been identified. Besides showing a broad base of groups interested in the historical markers, one wonders if today the sponsoring organizations still exist? If they do exist, do the current members realize their sponsorship? This becomes extremely important if a marker becomes damaged or lost. The real question becomes who replaces those markers?

In documenting the Maryland historic markers, care was taken to identify the sponsors. They are all listed in the back of the book. Each marker is referenced as to who the sponsor was by the numbers in parentheses at the end of the text.

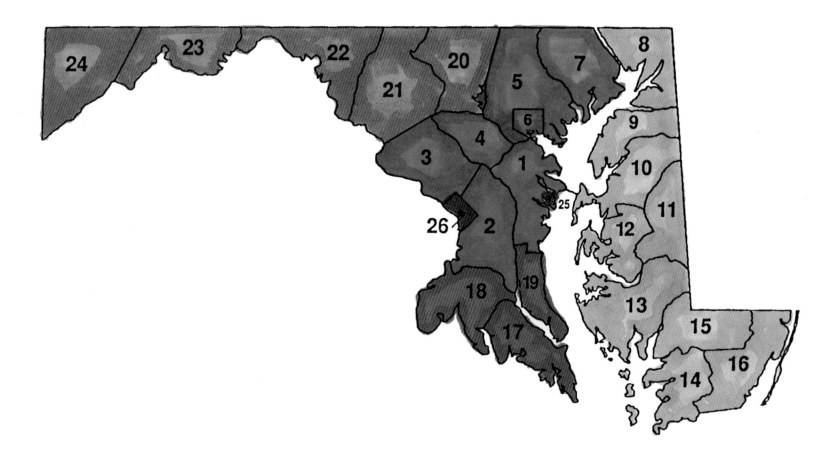

CENTRAL MARYLAND

1. Anne Arundel County

2. Prince George's County

3. Montgomery County

4. Howard County

5. Baltimore County

6. Baltimore City

7. Harford County

EASTERN SHORE

8. Cecil County

9. Kent County

10. Queen Anne's County

11. Caroline County

12. Talbot County

13. Dorchester County

14. Somerset County

15. Wicomico County

16. Worcester County

SOUTHERN MARYLAND

17. St. Mary's County

18. Charles County

19. Calvert County

WESTERN MARYLAND

20. Carroll County

21. Frederick County

22. Washington County

23. Allegany County

24. Garrett County

ADDITIONAL

25. Annapolis

26. Washington, D.C.

LOCATION

The next concern is the location of the markers. In this book, I started narrowing the locations by categorizing all the markers in either one of the 23 Maryland counties or the City of Baltimore. Further, at the end of the text of each marker is a brief description of the general location where one should be able to find the marker if it is still standing. I did not have the luxury of being able to travel to each location to verify the actual existence. Each area of the state has a map to help you locate all the markers in that area.

TEXT

The texts of the markers reproduced in this book are as accurate as possible. I did take some liberties in spelling certain obvious abbreviations. Many of the sentences in the text are very long, with little punctuation used. I tried to faithfully reproduce the text as written, but sometimes my sources were difficult to decipher. I left any gross misspellings as they were presented after checking the spelling many times with the originals I had to work from.

Occasionally during research on the markers, I came across the texts of some plaques attached to buildings, walls, monuments, etc., which were deemed important to the area being studied. I elected to include a few of the texts from the plaques in this book. For example, in Allegany County, I included the plaque texts on Col. Thomas Cresap and a few pertaining to buildings that played an important role during the Civil War. However, most of the texts in this book pertain to roadside markers.

The accuracy of the text of the markers could be questioned. Many of the markers refer to places or events that occurred hundreds of years earlier. Certainly there is room in this situation for errors to occur. However, the texts of the markers were developed by caring people who hoped to preserve for the future generations their most accurate recollections of times passed. With this in mind, the modern reader can capture a glimpse of our history from the markers in order to begin to form a reasonably accurate picture of our heritage. If one needs a more accurate truth, there are other research sources available to complete the picture.

HOW TO USE THIS BOOK

In each county and the City of Baltimore sections, I have attempted to alphabetize the markers based on the first important word in the title. The idea being if you were motoring down a street or highway and passed a marker, just read the first important word, then you could look up the text in the book rather rapidly without backtracking. Of course this assumes you know what county you are in at the time.

Each county and the City of Baltimore have a map which locates the approximate position of the markers. Each marker text is numbered with a number in a circle, which corresponds to the estimated location on the area map. Those marker numbers on the map with a red background are believed to be still standing. The marker numbers with a green background on the map are probably not still standing. The title of each marker is next and helps describe the site. The historic text follows. After the text is a number in parenthesis which designates the sponsoring organization. The sponsors can be found listed on page 130. The general location is described below this.

To challenge you as you search for and discover the fascinating information in the historical markers, there is a list of questions on page 128. Some examples of these are: Where was the capital of Maryland from 1634 to 1694? For whom was Fort McHenry named? The only answers given are the county or city where the correct answer can be found.

If any reader of this book finds a mistake in an existing marker's text or its location, please send the information to the author in care of: Image Publishing, Ltd., 1411 Hollins Street, Baltimore, Maryland 21223. Further, if anyone finds a historical plaque they think should be in future editions of this publication please send a copy of the text and location of the plaque to the address above.

For the first person who finds and notifies me of a legitimate Maryland roadside historical marker, not included in this book, I will send them a free copy of this book. The first person to notify me of a unique and significant plaque relating to Maryland history, which I deem to be important enough to add to future editions of this book, I will also send a free copy of this book.

ANNAPOLIS is located in Anne Arundel County and is the capitol of the State of Maryland. Pictured above is an aerial view with the Maryland State House in the circle at the center. The Governor's mansion is to the right of the State House. The boats at the top of the picture are located at the "foot" of Main Street on the South River which leads to the Chesapeake Bay.

ANNE ARUNDEL COUNTY

1 **Annapolis**

Capital of Maryland since 1695

Present State House begun 1772, where Continental Congress received Washington's resignation as Commander-in-Chief of the Continental Army 1783. Peggy Stewart Tea Party occurred 1774. Home of three signers of the Declaration of Independence. Hammond-Harwood house built 1774, (a period museum), St. John's College chartered 1784, U.S. Naval Academy founded 1845. (1)

U.S. 50 and 301, south of MD 70.
U.S. 50 and 301, at Mill Bottom Road.
MD 2, 1 mile north of Maceys Corner.

2 **Belvoir**

(Scott's Plantation)

French troops under Count De Rochambeau made their 36th camp here September 16-17, 1781, en route to Yorktown, Virginia. Most of the troops embarked from Annapolis, but the artillery marched to Georgetown to cross the Potomac River. (4)

MD 178, north of Honeysuckle Lane.

 3 **Birthplace of Johns Hopkins**

Founder of The Johns Hopkins University and The Johns Hopkins Hospital Medical School. Born May 19, 1795, died December 24, 1873. (4)

MD 3, at Evergreen Road.
MD 3, at Johns Hopkins Road.

4 **Butler in Annapolis**

The 8th Massachusetts Infantry reached Annapolis April 21, 1861, on the railroad ferry Maryland. Colonel Benjamin F. Butler forwarded his and the 7th New York Infantry Regiments to Washington. Shortly he was directed to prevent the legislature from acting on secession from the Union. (7)

U.S. Naval Academy Grounds, Santee Road at boat dock.

5 **Count De Rochambeau's**

Troops marched over this road from Spurrier's Tavern to "Scott's Plantation" (Belvoir) on September 16, 1781 on the way to Yorktown. Washington and Rochambeau had gone ahead September 10-11 on the way to Mt. Vernon. (1)

MD 178, south of Waterbury Road.

6 **Curtis Creek Furnace**

The Curtis Creek Furnace, located on the south side of Furnace Creek, one-half mile east of Ritchie Highway, was established in 1759 and, with a foundry built in 1829, continued to turn out high-grade charcoal pig iron until abandoned in 1851 (116)

MD 2, north of Furnace Branch Road.

 7 **The General's Highway**

Across the road stood the 3 mile oak under which General George Washington passed on his way to Annapolis, December 19, 1783 to resign his commission as Commander-in-Chief of the Continental Armies. According to tradition General Smallwood, General Gates and the distinguished Annapolis Citizens met Washington at this spot, 3 miles from the State House. General Lafayette on his return to America to visit with friends of Revolution days, passed here December 17, 1824. (118)

3 Mile Oak in front of bank on MD 450 and Generals Highway (MD 178).

8 **"The General's Highway"**

Route of George Washington's triumphant journey, December 3-23, 1783, New York to Annapolis, to resign as Commander-in-Chief of the first "American Army". (122)

MD 3

9 **The Governor Ritchie Highway**

(Formerly located at intersection. Presumably taken down when Ritchie Highway was widened, not standing as of 2-23-71.) (1)

MD 2, and Potee Street, at Baltimore City Line.

10 **Governor William Stone**

Born in England in 1603. Emigrated to Virginia circa 1640. Came to Maryland in 1647 bringing 33 settlers and was granted 5000 acres on the Servern River. Was made Lieutenant Governor by Lord Baltimore in 1648 with authority to enforce the Religious Toleration Act of 1649. He died on his Manor of Avon in Charles County in 1660. (123)

Governor Stone Parkway, north of Benfield Boulevard.

11 **Hammond-Harwood House**

Maryland Avenue at King George Street
Annapolis

Built 1774 by Matthias Hammond, local patriot. Designed by William Buckland, colonial architect. 18th century furnishings. One of America's famous houses. Open to the public. (120)

MD 70, 0.3 mile west of College Creek Bridge.

12 **Hockley-in-the-Hole**

(Patented August 25, 1664)

To Edward, Joshua, and John Dorsey, sons of Edward Dorsey who settled in Maryland in 1650. The patent was signed by Charles Calvert, then Lieutenant General, and later Third Lord Baltimore. This plantation had been the homestead of the Dorseys for over 300 years. (4)

MD 450 at Nichols Road.

13 **Holly Hill**

Surveyed, 1663, as Holland's Hills for Francis Holland; bought, 1665, by Richard Harrison, Quaker planter and ship owner, who owned about 6,000 acres. The house, built in three stages between 1665 and 1733 by Richard Harrison and his son Samuel, is one of the largest and best preserved of its period in Maryland. (4)

MD 261, east of Fairhaven Road.

14 **"Lafayette's Encampment"**

March - April 1781

During the Revolutionary War, 1200 Continental Light Infantryman under the command of the Marquis de Lafayette encamped on the rise behind this sign en route to the decisive battle in Yorktown, Virginia. They arrived in Annapolis from Head of Elk by a flotilla of Maryland ships under the command of Commodore James Nicholson. (124)

Annapolis

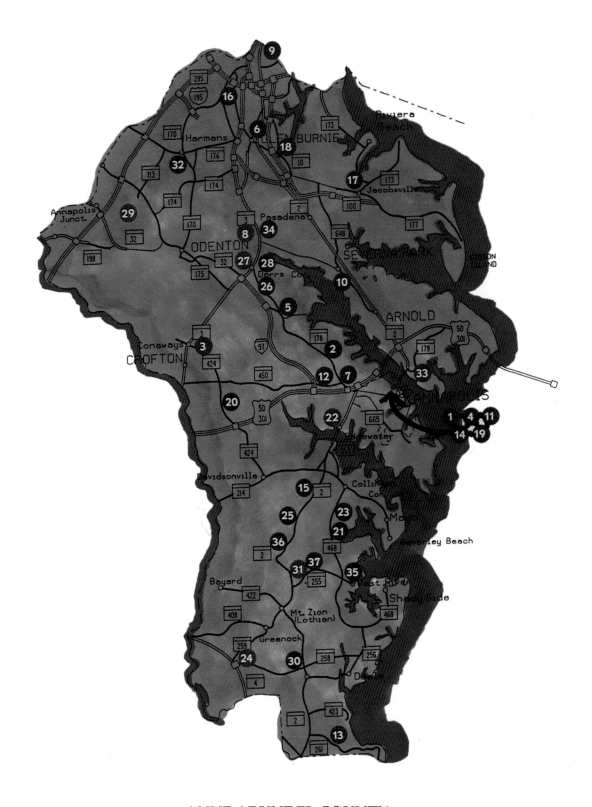

ANNE ARUNDEL COUNTY

Located directly south of Baltimore City and running along the edge of the Chesapeake Bay is
Anne Arundel County. The City of Annapolis has been the State Capital since 1695.

"Larkins Hills"
Patented 1663

Charles Lord Baltimore and his Council attended the Meeting of the Assembly here October 2 - November 6, 1683. 31 Towns and Ports of Entry were established at this session in the several counties along the bay. Practically none of these towns exist at the present time.   (1)

MD 2, 0.3 mile south of Mill Swamp Road.

Linthicum Heights
Side 1

Named after Abner Linthicum, Sr. (1763-1848), planter, Maryland legislator and Captain of the Anna Arundel County Militia, War of 1812. A descendant, Congressman John Charles Linthicum, born here in 1867, introduced and sponsored the bill Congress passed in 1931 which declared the Star Spangled Banner the National Anthem.

Holly Run Church

Built in 1828, Holly Run Church, an early Methodist Protestant Church in America, was restored in 1966.

Side 2

Benson - Hammond House

Built circa 1820, the Benson-Hammond House is the headquarters of the Anne Arundel County Historical Society and is open to the public.

Annapolis and Baltimore Short Line

Organized in 1880, the Annapolis and Baltimore Short Line ran its first steam-powered passenger train in 1887. It was purchased by the Washington, Baltimore and Annapolis Electric Railroad in 1921. The Linthicum depot was built in 1907 and restored in 1985.   (126)

MD 170, south of Twin Oaks Road.

Magothy Methodist Church

One of the first Methodist societies in Anne Arundel County. Log church originally erected on tract acquired in 1764, now the

cemetery. Bishop Francis Asbury preached here August 27, 1777. Church built on present site in 1859 was destroyed by fire in 1886. Rebuilt as it now stands, 1887.   (119)

MD 177, 0.3 mile west of MD 607.

Marley Chapel

Erected, 1731, near this site. Marley Chapel served as a Chapel of Ease for the northern parish area of St. Margaret's Episcopal Church. After its abandonment bricks from the chapel were used in constructing St. Alban's Episcopal Church, Glen Burnie, completed 1904.   (116)

MD 270 and MD 648.

Maryland State House
(built 1772 - 1779),
Capitol of the U.S.
November 26, 1783-August 13, 1784

In this State House, oldest in the nation still in legislative use, General George Washington resigned his commission before the Continental Congress December 23, 1783. Here, January 14, 1784, Congress ratified the Treaty of Paris to end the Revolutionary War and, May 7, 1784, appointed Thomas Jefferson Minister Plenipotentiary. From here, September 14, 1786, the Annapolis Convention issued the call to the states that led to the Constitutional Convention.   (4)

4 Identical markers, one each at north, south, east and west entrances to the State House, Annapolis.

Middle Plantation

600 Acres patented in 1664 to Mareen Duvall, Esq., great Huguenot and native of France. Appointed Commissioner for Advancement of Trade 1683. He died here 1694. The plantation remained the ancestral seat of a junior branch of the Duvall family for many years.   (121)

MD 424, 0.2 mile north of Rossback Road.

Old Quaker Burying Ground
1672

Here April, 1672, George Fox, founder of Quakerism, opened the first general meeting of Friends in Maryland, marking the

beginning of West River Yearly Meeting and its successor, Baltimore Yearly Meeting of Friends. Site of West River Quaker Meeting House. (4)

MD 255 and MD 468.

The Old South River Club

Organized 1720. House built 1742. The oldest Social Club in America (first road to the left).   (1)

MD 2 and South River Club House Road.

Overlooking West River
(1st) Cedar Park - (2nd) Tulip Hill

Cedar Park - patented to Richard Ewen in 1666 as "Ewen upon Ewenton." Brick house built c. 1697 by Richard Galloway II around earlier frame structure possibly dating back to 1656. Known as "W. River Farm" in 18th Century. Home and burial place of John Francis Mercer, 10th Governor of Maryland (1801-1803). Tulip Hill - patented 1659 to Richard Talbott as "Poplar Knowle." Brick house built circa 1756 by Samuel Galloway, Quaker merchant. George Washington recorded visits there September 22 and 30, 1771, traveling to and from races at Annapolis.   (12)

MD 255, east of MD 468.

Portland Manor
Surveyed December 6, 1667

Portland Landing and Saint Jerome's, surveyed 1700, owned by Colonel Henry Darnall, brother-in-law of Charles, 3rd Lord Baltimore and Secretary of State. Parts of this property have never left the Darnell Family and are now owned (1938) by one of the descendants.   (1)

MD 4, at road to Greenock.

Rawlings Tavern

Jonathan Raulings given a license to keep an "ordinary" (tavern) 1771. George Washington dined here September 26, 1773, on his way to the Annapolis Races.   (1)

MD 2 and Harwood Road.

The Severn Crossroads Church

Built as a Methodist Church in 1861, but used

Paca House and Gardens

Hammond-Harwood House

Paca House Interior

Hammond-Harwood House

PACA HOUSE AND GARDENS - This Georgian mansion was built between 1763 and 1765 by William Paca. William Paca was one of the signers of the Declaration of Independence and later became Governor of the State of Maryland. **HAMMOND-HARWOOD HOUSE** - The Hammond-Harwood House is Georgian in style and is one of the finest examples of late Colonial architecture in America.

on alternated Sundays by Episcopalians for fifty years. Moved in 1896 from southeast to northeast corner of General's Highway and Indian Landing Roads, and dedicated in 1935 to Charles W. Baldwin, its pastor for 71 years. The Severn Crossroads Foundation moved it to its present site in 1981. (125)

Millersville Road, northwest from General Highway, Millersville.

27 Shipley's Choice

Adam Shipley came to Anne Arundel County in 1668. On March 30, 1681, 200 acres were surveyed and patented in his name. This tract was the earliest patented in the Shipley name. Dedicated during the development of the subdivision named in his honor. (123)

Benfield Boulevard, west of Scarlett Oak Drive.

28 Shipley Choice

Adam Shipley, who came to Anne Arundel County in 1668, on March 30, 1681, patented 200 acres on the south side of the Severn River. Dedicated during the Tercentenary Commemoration of the Shipley's of Maryland, May 25, 1968. (4)

MD 3, 0.1 mile south of the Severn River Bridge.

29 Site of Ellicott's Chapel
(Episcopal)
Queen Caroline Parish 1840-1868

St. Peter's Parish Church 1869-1917. Included in Military Reservation and used as a Chapel 1917-1919. (117)

St. Peter's Church near Ft. Meade Cemetery No. 9.

30 St. James' Church
Old Herring Creek Parish

The first church on this site was built, 1695, and the present structure was completed 1765. The Reverend Henry Hall (1675-1722) served as first rector, 1698-1722. From 1786-1792 Saint James' was the home parish of Thomas John Claggett (1743-1816), first Protestant Episcopal Bishop of

Maryland and first to be consecrated in America. (4)

MD 2, 0.3 mile north of MD 258.

31 Tulip Hill

Land patented, 1659, to Richard Talbott as "Poplar Knowle". George Washington "dined at Mr. Sam Galloway's" September 22, 1771, en route to the races at Annapolis and "dined and supped" here on his return trip September 30, 1771. (4)

MD 2, Owensville.

Side One
32 Wesley Grove United Methodist Church

Consecrated Sunday, November 4, 1951, by the joint congregations of Friendship and Ridge Methodist Churches.

Timber Ridge and Friendship Methodist Church

Timber Ridge Church was built circa 1840 two miles to the east of here. It was disbanded in 1869 when southern sympathizers built Friendship Church across the road. A new Friendship Church was built on the former Timber Ridge site in 1900 and was last used for worship on Easter, 1948, before being razed for construction of Friendship Airport (now BWI).

Side Two
Wesley Grove United Methodist Church

Consecrated Sunday, November 4, 1951, by the joint congregations of Friendship and Ridge Methodist Churches.

Prospect Hill and Ridge Methodist Churches

Prospect Hill Church was built circa 1840, one mile to the west on land known as The Wilderness. In 1866 the southern sympathizers abandoned the building which fell in ruins and built Ridge Chapel at Shipley's Grove. A new sanctuary was built adjoining the old church in 1892, and is in use today as a church. (116)

1320 Dorsey Road (MD 176), Harmons.

33 White Hall

The colonial country home of Governor Horatio Sharpe (1718 - 1790) next to the last Colonial Governor of the Province of Maryland 1753-1768. House built about 1764. Owned by Ridout Family 1782-1895. Considered the finest example of Maryland colonial houses. (1)

MD 450 and MD 648.

34 Widow Ramsey's Tavern

Near here was junction of Old Baltimore-Annapolis Road ("The General's Highway") and a road laid out by Charles Carroll from Doughoregan Manor. On the south side of Severn Run stood Widow Ramsey's where George Washington breakfasted June 7, 1773, and again on May 6, 1775, as he traveled north to take command of the Revolutionary Forces. (5)

MD 3 at Dicus Mill Road.

35 William Penn

Attended a meeting of the Friends (Quakers) at Thomas Hooker's December 1682 on this tract called "Brownton" (patented in 1652 for 660 acres). Penn sailed from here across the bay to the Choptank River to a General Meeting of the Friends. (1)

MD 255, 1 mile east of MD 468.

36 William Penn

Came here to the home of Colonel Thomas Tailler on "The Ridge" December 13, 1682 for his first conference with Charles Lord Baltimore as to the location of the boundary line between Maryland and Pennsylvania. (1)

MD 2, 1 mile north of Harwood.

37 William Penn

Visited his Quaker Friend William Richardson near this spot after the conference at Colonel Thomas Tailler's December 13, 1682. Lord Baltimore and the members of his Council accompanied him to this place. (1)

MD 255, 1.7 miles west of MD 468.

CALVERT MANSION - This mansion was the home of George Calvert who on June 11, 1799 married, Rosalie Eugenie, the daughter of a Belgian Baron Henri Joseph Stier. The mansion is a replica of an 18th century Belgian mansion and was a gift to the newlyweds by Baron Stier. (See page 25, marker 38).

PRINCE GEORGE'S COUNTY

1 Abraham Lincoln

This statue of the Great Emancipator portrays in his last days the thin, tired, war-torn President in thoughtful and deep meditation and is considered one of the finest bronze statues ever made of President Lincoln. It was created by one of America's foremost sculptors, Andrew O'Connor, who also did the Statue of Lincoln which stands in front of the State House in Springfield Illinois. It was cast by the Gorham Manufacturing Company of Providence, Rhode Island, in the most permanent medium that nature has given man, enduring bronze.   (150)

In Fort Lincoln Cemetery off Bladensburg Road.

2 Adelphia Mill

This old grist mill built in the summer of 1796, probably by two brothers Issacher and Mahlon Scofield. In 1811 the mill was also used for wool carding. The Miller's cottage is of the same period.   (142)

MD 212, north of the bridge and south of the park entrance.

3 Beall's Pleasure

Patented 1706

Built 1795 by Benjamin Stoddert, first Secretary of the Navy, 1798-1801. A Revolutionary War Major, Stoddert was born 1751 in Charles County and died here December 18, 1813. Land originally granted to Colonel Niniam Beall of Georgetown. (4)

MD 202 near Old Landover Road.

4 Belair Mansion

Belair was built circa 1740 by Samuel Ogle, Governor of Maryland. Through the years the mansion became known as the "House of Governors" because Governors Thomas Bladder, Benjamin Tasker, Sr., Benjamin Ogle I, Oden Bowie and Christopher Lowndes were also associated with it at different times.   (4)

MD 197 and Tulip Grove Road.

5 The Belair Stud Farm

Cradle of American Racing

Colonial manor where breeding for the turf was carried on for three centuries, laying the foundation of American thoroughbred racing. Samuel Ogle, original owner, imported the stallion "Spark", the filly "Queen Mab" and other prize horses. His brother-in-law, Benjamin Tasker, Jr., continuing family tradition, bred "Othello" and "Selima", prides of the colonies. Belair Stud Farm blood flows in the veins of almost every American race horse of distinction. William Woodward, Sr., last private owner, fielded triple crown winners "Gallant Fox", 1930, and "Omaha", 1935. Operation of the farm continued until 1955.   (4)

MD 450 and Belair Drive.

6 Bellefields

Formerly Sim's Delight

Built circa 1720 by Dr. Patrick Sim who fled Scotland after the 1715 rebellion to settle in this country where, 1718, he married Mary, daughter of Thomas and Barbara Dent Brooke, of nearby Brookfield Manor. Colonel Joseph Sim, their oldest son, born here, died November 27, 1793. He was a Justice of the Supreme Court, and one of the Annapolis Assembly which, June 22, 1774, denounced the British closing of Boston Harbor. He represented his country June, 1775, at the Annapolis Convention which formed the Association of Freemen of Maryland. He served in the Convention of Maryland which governed the State at the beginning of the Revolution, and on the first Privy Council of the State, 1777. He was also a member of the General Assembly, 1780.   (4)

Entrance road to Bellefields Estate, Croom

7 Birthplace of John Carroll

Born 1755 Died 1815

First Archbishop in United States, 1808. At request of Congress in 1776 he accompanied Benjamin Franklin, Samuel Chase, and Charles Carroll of Carrollton to Quebec in an effort to have Canada unite with the Thirteen Colonies in the Revolution. Founder of Georgetown College, 1789.   (1)

Main street between E and W Streets, Upper Marlboro.

8 Bladensburg

(Named for Thomas Bladen)
Governor of Maryland, 1742-47

Brother George Washington and Martha Washington often here from 1751-1798. He "lodged" here going to Georgetown where, on March 30, 1791, Prince George's County ceded most of the new National Capital. Scene, Battle of Bladensburgh, 1814. Brother Lafayette here, 1824 .   (151)

MD 40 and U.S. 50.

9 Calvert Manor

Originally a grant of 3,000 acres by Cecil Calvert, second Lord Baltimore, to his nephew, William Calvert, 1662. The area was visited by Captain John Smith, 1608, by Captain Henry Fleet, 1629, and by Governor Leonard Calvert and father Andrew White, 1634.   (4)

Farmington Road, east of Wannas Road.

10 Cheltenham United Methodist Church

Formerly
Westwood Methodist Episcopal Church

Founded in 1873 at Westwood Farm, home of Julius H. Pyles. The cornerstone was laid on October 30, 1879 and the church constructed by the congregation. Enoch Pratt, Baltimore City philanthropist, attended the dedication. The pulpit was handmade from a cherry tree taken from the property. Early ministers traveled from Bladensburg on horseback. The Sunday School building was added in 1945.   (149)

U.S. 301 in church yard south of Frank Tippett Road.

11 Christ Episcopal Church

Accokeek

Erected in 1745 when it was declared by the General Assembly of Maryland to be the "Lower Chapel of Ease" for King George's (Piscataway) Parish. Christ Church was the outgrowth of a Chapel established about 1698 by private contributions. In 1823 it received recognition as a "separate" congregation and in 1869 became the Parish Church of St. John's Parish. In 1856 this

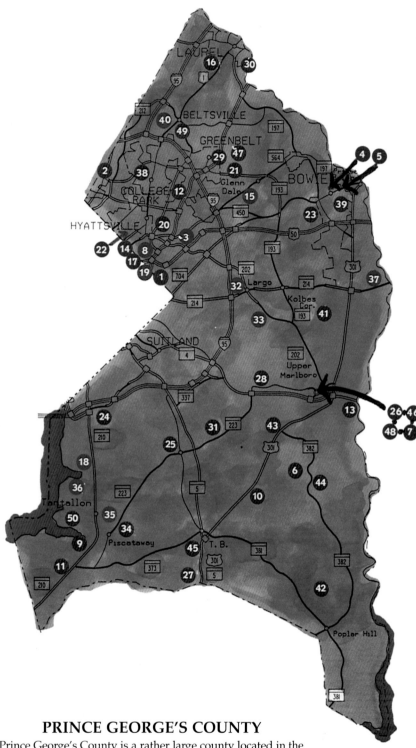

PRINCE GEORGE'S COUNTY

Prince George's County is a rather large county located in the
southern part of Central Maryland. It is bordered by the Patuxent
River and Anne Arundel County on the east and Washington,
D.C. on the south and west. The influence of the nation's capital
can be seen throughout the county.

structure was destroyed by fire, but was
rebuilt in 1857. (149)
Byran Point and Farmington Road.

12 College Park Airport

"Oldest continually operated in the World"
First Military Airfield in the U.S.

1907 - early aeronautical experiments by
Rex Smith and others; 1909 October 8,
Wilbur Wright instructed first flying offi-
cers of the Signal Corps, U.S. Army; 1909 -
October 29, Mrs. Ralph H. Van Demon first
woman passenger in America; 1911 - July 3,
First Army Flying School established; 1912
- First Flight Surgeon Lieutenant John P.
Kelly; 1912 - first group cross country flight
originated were first long distance flight -
42 miles, designation, Chevy Chase,
Maryland. First bombs dropped from an
aircraft utilizing a bombsight. (149)
*North end Colonel Frank S. Scott Drive off
Calvert Road between U.S. 1 and MD 201.*

13 Commodore Joshua Barney

Ordered upstream when a British fleet under
Admiral Cockburn entered the Patuxent,
Barney disembarked his Naval force of 500
men near here. August 21, 1814, burned his
vessels, and marched to help in the defense of
Washington. The sunken remains of his flotil-
la - a cutter, a gunboat and 13 barges - were
found near this bridge in the early 1900's. (4)
*MD 4 just west of the bridge of Anne
Arundel County line.*

14 Dueling Grounds

On this site, now part of Anacostia River
Park, more than 50 duels were fought during
the first half of the 19th Century. Here, on
what became known as "the dark and
bloody grounds," gentlemen of Washington
settled their political and personal differ-
ences. One of the most famous disputes was
that between Commodores Stephen Decatur
and James Barron, which was settled here on
March 22, 1820. Commodore Decatur, who
had gained fame as the conqueror of the
Barbary Pirates, was fatally wounded by his

antagonist. Although Congress passed an antidueling law in 1839, duels continued here until just before the Civil War. (146)

Alt. U.S. 1 just north of Lincoln Cemetery, near district line.

15 The First Agricultural College

And experimental farm in western hemisphere. Started 1854 by the Maryland State Agricultural Society through private subscriptions to stock. Chartered and enlarged by the Maryland Legislature 1856. Merged with the University of Maryland 1920. (1)

On Washington Boulevard, in front of Dairy Building of the Agricultural College.

16 The First Telegram
"What Hath God Wrought"

Was sent from Capitol in Washington to Baltimore May 24, 1844 over wires laid along the right of way of the B & O Railroad adjacent to this highway. The telegraph was invented by Samuel F. B. Morse (1791-1872). (1)

U.S. 1, south of Muirkirk Road.

17 Fort Lincoln

These earthworks are a portion of the original fortifications which made up Fort Lincoln. This fort was built during the summer of 1861 to serve as an outer defense of the City of Washington. It was named in honor of President Lincoln by General Order number 18, A.G.O., September 30, 1861. The Brigade of Major General Joseph Hooker was the first to occupy this area. In immediate command of the Fort was Captain T. S. Paddock. The Civil War cannons have been placed here through the courtesy of the Department of Defense to commemorate this auspicious occasion. (150)

Fort Lincoln Cemetery near Bladensburg Road.

18 Fort Washington
Originally Fort Warburton

Site chosen by George Washington on the approach of the British vessels August 23, 1814. The Fort was abandoned without firing a shot and the magazine was blown up by the officer in command. Rebuilt at order of President Madison by Major L'Enfant. (1)

MD 224 at Selisia.

19 George Washington

First entered Prince George's County (as now constituted) at this point August 1761 and made his last exit therefrom December 18, 1798. (152)

MD 40 at District of Columbia Line.

20 George Washington House
circa 1752

The George Washington House, often referred to as the Indian Queen Tavern, was built by tavern keeper Jacob Wirt. Prior to the Revolution when Bladensburg was a thriving port town, this building was rented out to Dunningham and Company, a Scottish mercantile firm, which traded in tobacco. The building later served as a tavern and stagecoach stop for weary travelers during their journeys along the Old Post Road, a major route linking the north and south. (149)

Upshur Street, Alt. U.S. 1.

21 Greenbelt
1937

Greenbelt was the 1st of 3 planned garden towns built and owned by the U.S. Government during the Administration of President Franklin D. Roosevelt. It was a "new deal" experiment in community planning, of note to urban planners throughout the world. The 885 original homes were built in a series of clusters, joined by interior walks, and circling central business, civic and recreation facilities. Greenbelt incorporated September 1, 1937 as the 1st Maryland City with a Council-Manager Government. (149)

Southway, north of the off ramp from Baltimore-Washington Parkway.

22 "Hitching Post Hill"
or "Ash Hill"

George Calvert sold this land, 1836, to Robert Clark, builder of the house, 1840. General Edward F. Beale, early surveyor and government agent in the southwest, bought the estate, 1875. Presidents Grant and Cleveland were frequent visitors as was "Buffalo Bill" Cody. Grant's Arabian Horses were kept on the land. (4)

Rosemary Lane, University Parkway, Hyattsville.

23 Holy Trinity Church

The original house of worship on this site, part of "Martha's Choice", was a Chapel of Ease. It was donated to Queen Anne's Parish by the Reverend Jacob Henderson and his wife Mary, widow of Mareen Duvall, Esquire. In 1844 it became Holy Trinity Parish. (121)

MD 450, west of High Bridge Road.

24 John Hanson

President of the United States in Congress assembled, 1781-82. Died November 15, 1783, at "Oxon Hill". 1^{1}/$_{2}$ miles west of here, the original mansion house, built by the Addison Family, was burned February 6, 1895. (1)

MD 414 east of MD 210 at High School Annex, near Oxen Hill.

25 John Wilkes Booth

The assassin of Lincoln stopped here at the house of Mrs. Surratt to secure ammunition on the night of April 14, 1865. He rode on to "T.B" and then to Dr. Mudd's who set his broken leg. (1)

Brandywine Road, just south of MD 223 (on grounds), Clenton.

26 Marlborough
(County Seat of Prince George's Since 1721)

George Washington "lodged" here August 31, 1774, going to First Continental Congress, May 4, 1775, on his way to second Continental Congress where, on June 15, 1775, he was elected "General and Commander-in-Chief of the Army of the United Colonies." His first visit here was as

BELAIR MANSION - The Belair mansion was built, circa 1740, by Samuel Ogle. It has become known as the "House of Governors" because the number of governors which were associated with it through the years. (See page 21, markers 4 and 5).

Colonel of Virginia Militia in 1756 and his last as President of the United States in 1793. (143)
Main Street and Old Marlboro Pike, Upper Marlboro.

 Mattawoman Run
Charles and Prince George's Counties

Named for the Mattawoman Indians who had a fort and town in this locality. In 1670 Governor Charles Calvert presented to their King Maquata, a medal with the likeness of his father Cecilius, Second Lord Baltimore, on one side and a map of Maryland on the other. A replica is in the possession of the Maryland Historical Society. (1)
U.S. 301 and MD 5, south of Prince George's County Line.

 "Melwood Park"
Patented 1672

The home of Ignatius Digges, whose daughter, Mary, married Thomas Sim Lee, twice Governor of Maryland. Lee died here, 1819. General George Washington visited here four times and Martha Washington once. In the war of 1812 British officers stopped here briefly. (4)
Old Marlboro Pike, 0.7 mile east of MD 223.

 Methodist Preaching Place
1776-1803

Bishop Francis Asbury, builder of Methodism in America, recorded nine visits to this place. The farm, called "Wild Cat', belonged to Shadrick Turner, planter. He and wife Sarah, zealous laymen, hosted many meetings. Several United Methodist Churches of Prince George's County stem from this early preaching. Nearby is the Turner Family Graveyard, the only remains of "Wild Cat". In 1941 the property was deeded to the City of Greenbelt to be a part of the City Cemetery. (149)
MD 201, north of Crescent Road.

 Montpelier

The home of Major Snowden, original grant 1686. George Washington stopped here May 9 and September 21, 1787, on his way

to and returning from the Constitutional Convention. (140)
MD 197 and Montpelier Drive, Laurel.

 "Mount Airy"

17th century hunting lodge of the Lords Baltimore. 9200 acres acquired in 1751 by the Honorable Benedict Calvert member of the Council, son of Charles, fifth Lord Baltimore. Here, with George Washington present February 4, 1774, Benedict's daughter "Nelly" married John Parke Custis, son of Martha Washington. Birthplace of George Washington Parke Custis, their son, who married Mary Lee Fitzhugh and built "Arlington" on the Potomac. (4)
Rosaryville Road and Dower House Road.

 "Mount Lubentia"
(Patented by Ninian Beall as"Largo", 1686)

Known as "Castle Magruder", where lived Reverend Jonathan Boucher, tutor to "Jackie" Custis. George and Martha Washington, Nelly and John Parke Custis, Benedict Calvert and Robert Eden, last Royal Governor of Maryland, were here September 4-5, 1772. Washington was also here September 6, 7, October 4, 10, 1772 and April 12, 1773. (143)
MD 202 (Largo - Landover Road) at entrance to house.

 Northampton

Patented to Thomas Sprigg 1673. House erected 1704, added to 1788, burnt 1909. Washington stopped September 7, 1772 and September 29, 1773. Home of Samuel Sprigg, Governor of Maryland 1819 - 1822. Visited by Lafayette October 24, 1824. Birthplace of Lord Fairfax, 12th Baron of Cameron, only American born member of British House of Lord's. (1)
On U.S. 50.

 Piscataway

Named for the local Indian Tribe. Washington passed many times on his way to and from Mount Vernon across the Potomac. (1)
MD 223 at Floral Park Road.

 Piscataway

Site of an Indian Village to which Governor Leonard Calvert sailed up the Potomac River on "The Dove" in 1634 and visited the Emperor of the Piscataways before determining upon a permanent settlement at St. Mary's. (1)
MD 210 and Farmington Road

 Prince George's County St. John's Church

Erected 1723. (King George's Parish established 1692). Credible evidence and honest tradition record that Washington attended services here on numerous occasions. (145)
Church grounds, on Broadcreek Road.

 Queen Anne, Maryland
(2 miles distant)

A "Porte Towne" in 1707. Washington was at Boyd's Tavern there September 1, 1774 and March 27, 1791. (148)
MD 214, west of Anne Arundel County Line.

 Riversdale

Site of the gates at the original entrance to Riversdale, or the Calvert Mansion. Built 1800-1803 by Baron Henri Joseph Stier of Belgium, as a wedding gift for his daughter Rosalie Eugenie who married George Calvert, June 11, 1799. (4)
U.S. 1 between Oliver and Harrison Streets.

Sacred Heart Chapel
White Marsh
(formerly St. Frances Borgia)

Sacred Heart Chapel was built about 1741 by Jesuit priests on the property known as White Marsh. The priests turned their 2,000 acre bequest into a thriving plantation. During the 1780's the American Clergy met several times at White Marsh, and here on May 18th, 1789 they nominated John Carroll to be the first American Bishop. In the 1800's Jesuit Novices studied at White Marsh, including Pierre De Smet, missionary to the Indians. On Pentecost, 1853, fire destroyed everything on the hill except the wall. (149)
MD 450, east of Race Track Road.

MONTPELIER MANSION - was built in the 1770's and was the home of Major Snowden. It has been preserved by the state because of its historic and architectural beauty. (See page 25, marker 30).

40 Site of Rhodes Tavern

Lieutenant-General George Washington "dined at Rhodes" December 18, 1798 on his last journey from Philadelphia to Mount Vernon. (141)

U.S. 1 near Beltsville.

41 St. Barnabas Church

Erected, 1774, (Queen Anne Parish, established, 1705), in Prince George's County. In the church which preceded this present structure, George Washington and Robert Eden, last Royal Governor of Maryland, attended service, September 6, 1772, Reverend Johnathan Boucher, Rector. (144)

Church Road, and Oak Grove Road, Leeland.

42 St. Pauls Episcopal Church
Baden - Founded 1692

Parish Church of St. Paul's Parish, one of the 30 original Parishes established in 1692 in the Province of Maryland. The present structure was built in 1733 to replace the earlier church at Mount Calvert that was in existence prior to 1692. The right Reverend Thomas John Claggett, D.D., first Episcopal Bishop consecrated in America, served as Rector of the Parish following the American Revolution while he was Bishop of Maryland. (149)

Horsehead Road and Baden Westwood Roads.

43 St. Thomas Episcopal Church of Croome
1732

Originally a Chapel of Ease in St. Paul's Parish, Prince George's County. The church was once the charge of the Right Reverend Thomas Claggett, First Protestant Episcopal Bishop consecrated in America. Members of the Calvert Family, proprietors of Colonial Maryland, are buried here. (4)

U.S. 301 and Croome Road (MD 382).

44 St. Thomas' Parish Church
Side #1

Successor to the 17th Century Anglican Church at Mount Calvert, this cruciform, brick church was authorized in 1732 and completed in 1745 during the rectorate of John Eversfield, 1728-1780. Built by Daniel Page it served as Chapel of Ease for the northern part of St. Paul's Parish, Prince George's County, until 1850. Since 1850 it has been parish church of St. Thomas' Parish, Prince George's County.

Side #2

Victorianized in the 1850's, it was partially restored following the detailed original contract 1955-58. Thomas John Claggett, first Bishop of Maryland, lived near here and served as priest in this church. Members of the Lord Proprietor's family are buried here. Always open for prayer and worship. The Blessed Sacrament has been continuously reserved many years. (147)

St. Thomas' Church Road and Croome road (MD 382).

45 T.B.
Initials on a Boundary Stone which stood near this point and marked the corner of "Brookefield"

A tract of 2530 acres patented in 1664 to Thomas Brooke, 1632-1676. Member of the Maryland Assembly 1663-76; presiding Justice County Court 1667; Major in Forces fighting Indians 1667. (1)

MD 5, just south of MD 373.

46 Thomas John Claggett, D.D.

Ordained by Lord Bishop of London 1768. First Bishop consecrated in the United States, at Trinity Church, New York City by Bishop Seabury of Connecticut. He organized this (Trinity) Church 1810. Born near Nottingham October 3, 1743, died at "Croom" August 3, 1816. (1)

Church Street on Church grounds, Upper Marlboro.

47 Toaping Castle
circa 1750

On this site Isaac, Charles and Nathan Walker erected a large white oak log house named for their ancestral stronghold in Scotland which the three brothers had fled after the failure of attempts to unseat George I King of England as ruler of Scotland. Isaac permanently settled here and obtained land grants for 100 acres. He and his three sons served in the Revolutionary War. The graves of Isaac and his son Nathan are north of here. Toaping Castle was the birth place of Samuel Hamilton Walker (February 24, 1817-October 8, 1847) Lt. Colonel of the Texas Rangers and Captain of the U.S. Cavalry. He left home at age 19 to fight Indians and later he became a leader and hero of the Rangers. His suggested changes to Samuel Colt's revolver resulted in Colt's success as an arms manufacturer. 1000 Colt-Walker pistols - the first, heaviest and longest revolvers ever issued to American forces - were purchased for Texas Rangers during the Mexican War. Walker was killed in that war at the Battle of Hua Mantla, Mexico. The family cemetery is all that remains of the Toaping Castle estate. (149)

Walker Drive, north of MD 193, in Greenbelt.

48 Tomb of Dr. William Beanes

To Secure the release of prisoners of war Dr. Beanes and Francis Scott Key visited the British Fleet, September, 1814. Detained until after the attack on Baltimore, the two witnessed the bombardment of Fort McHenry on the 13th and 14th during which Key was inspired to write "The Star-Spangled Banner." (4)

MD 4 near Water Street, Upper Marlboro.

49 Van Horn's Tavern

On Vansville Hill, Prince George's County, Maryland. President George Washington stopped there July 19, August 7 and September 12, 1795. (4)

U.S. 1, north of MD 212, Beltsville.

50 "Warburton Manor"
Patented 1661

Home of the Digges Family. (Descendants of Edward Digges, Governor of Virginia, 1652 -1668). The most intimate friends of George and Martha Washington in Prince George's County, where they visited many times. Washington spent his forty-third birthday here. Now site of Fort Washington, designed by L'Enfant, 1814. (143)

In Fort Washington Park, MD 210.

Great Falls

C&O Canal, Great Falls Tavern

Clara Barton House

White's Ferry

GREAT FALLS - The Potomac River quietly flows along most of the length of Maryland's southern border. In the area around Great Falls the river drops rapidly forming a turbulent, white water paradise. **C&O CANAL - GREAT FALLS TAVERN** - Located at Great Falls, the tavern is located along the tow path of the C&O Canal. **CLARA BARTON HOUSE** - This house was the early headquarters of the American Red Cross and the home of Clara Barton, its founder. **WHITE'S FERRY** - An important old ferry used in the Civil War by General Lee's Army and others. The ferry is still in operation today.

MONTGOMERY COUNTY

1   **August 26, 1814**

In this village President Madison and members of his official family found refuge in the home of Caleb Bentley, first Postmaster of Brookeville, following the burning of the Capitol and the White House by the British Army. Many other refugees from Washington also found shelter here. Erected August 22, 1964.   (111)

MD 97 (S. High Street) at Market Street, Brookeville.

2 **Chesapeake and Ohio Aqueduct**

Across the Monacacy River

Largest of eleven C & O Aqueducts, finished 1833. Alfred Cruger principal engineer. Constructed of quartzite from Sugarloaf Mountain. It served until 1924, when after a flood, commercial operation ceased. Administered by the National Park Service.   (1)

MD 28 near Dickerson.

3 **The Civil War at Poolesville**

Famed Commander Lieutenant Colonel E.V. ("Lige") White of the 35th Battalion, Virginia Cavalry C.S.A. and many members of his command were natives of this area. This town became the headquarters of Union Brigadier General Charles P. Stone's 12,000-man Corps of Observation from June 1861, until March 1862. Four regiments from this command fought at Balls Bluff on the Virginia side of the Potomac six miles from this sign, on October 21, 1861. Colonel Edward Baker of Oregon, was killed and funeral services were held here. Major General Hooker's Headquarters were established here on June 26, 1863, during the Gettysburg Campaign. Skirmishes occurred here in September, November and December 1862 and July 1864.   (115)

Poolesville.

4 **The Clara Barton House**

Early headquarters of the American Red Cross and home of Clara Barton, founder and first President, who lived here until her death in 1912. Located just south of this marker, the house has an unusual interior of steamboat gothic design with railed galleries and a suspended captain's room.   (111)

MacArthur Boulevard at MD 614, Glen Echo.

5   **Damascus**

The "Town of Damascus" was founded in 1816. This marker stands on one of the original 14 lots laid out by the founder and first Postmaster, Edward Hughes. The earliest part of the town was located in the southwestern corner of "the Pleasant Plains of Damascus." A 1,101 acre tract patented by Matthew Pigman in 1774. (113)

MD 108 and Woodfield Road.

6 **Daniel Carroll of Rock Creek**

July 22, 1730 - May 7, 1796

Near this spot was the home of Daniel Carroll, member of the Second Continental Congress and of the Federal Constitutional Convention. He was a representative from Maryland in the first United States Congress and served as one of the three Commissioners who surveyed the District of Columbia.   (111)

MD 192 and Rosensteel Avenue, Silver Spring.

7 **Early Blacksmith Shop**

Originally a blacksmith shop, this home was built in the middle of the eighteenth century. It stands on a tract once known as "Magruder's Honesty". Believed to have been built by Ninian Magruder, senior (?-1751), it is one of the oldest standing structures in Montgomery County.   (4)

MD 190 and Seven Locks Road. Bethesda.

8   **Edwards Ferry**

This crossing was guarded by Union Troops during the Civil War. In October, 1861, Union Troops crossed here during the Ball's Bluff Operation, but did not participate in the battle. In June, 1863, the major part of the Union Army crossed on the way to Gettysburg, Pennsylvania.   (7)

East of Edward and Ferry Road on River Road.

9   **Elton**

Birthplace of Ridgely Brown, CSA 1833-1864

May 15, 1862, with seventeen young Marylanders he organized first Maryland Calvary. He served consistently and gallantly, rising from private to Lieutenant Colonel. Killed at South Anna River, Virginia, June 1, 1864.   (112)

MD 97, north of MD 650, Sunshine.

10   **Fort Sumner**

Forts Alexander, Ripley and Franklin, built to protect the Washington water system in 1861, were connected by earthworks in 1863 and renamed Fort Sumner to honor Major General Edwin V. Sumner, a hero of Antietam. The Fort's 28 cannon provided a formidable bulwark against raiding Confederates. Nothing remains of the Fort but an outline of it appears on the reverse.   (155)

Sangamore Road and Westpath Way, Bethesda.

11 **General Edward Braddock**

In April 1755, accompanied by Governor Horatio Sharpe of Maryland, traveled this road in a coach and six horses, on his way to Frederick, Maryland, to meet Benjamin Franklin and George Washington, to arrange for teams for the Fort Duquesne Expedition.   (1)

MD 355, north of Summit Avenue, Gaithersburg.

12 **Great Falls of the Potomac**

One of the most picturesque spots in Maryland. George Washington came here many times and built a canal lock on the Virginia side to make the river navigable for his "Potomac Company".   (1)

River Road and Bradley Lane.

MONTGOMERY COUNTY

Montgomery County is a transition county between the urban eastern area of the county which borders Washington, D.C., to the mostly rural countryside of the western part of the county. One of the most affluent counties in the state and nation, it has the largest per capita income in Maryland.

13 ### Jubal Early's Raid on Washington

The only contingent of Confederate Soldiers to enter Washington during the Civil War marched down Georgia Avenue formerly called Seventh Street Pike, the 11th and 12th of July, 1864, and attacked Fort Stevens. President Lincoln arrived at Fort Stevens to witness the fray and narrowly escaped a Confederate bullet, the only president under enemy fire during his term in office. Hastily summoned Union reinforcements under Generals Horatio Wright and Frank Wheaton arrived from Petersburg, Virginia on July 13th. Early's troops retreated, having failed to capture Washington. The battle left nearly 300 men dead, wounded or missing.   (114)

Woodside Park - Spring Street and Georgia Avenue (MD 97)

14 ### Montgomery County Game Refuge

76 Acres, purchased November 16, 1925, from William S. and Elizabeth Caulfield, and Aldelaide Welti, from Hunter's License Fund, for the purpose of propagating game.   (3)

U.S. 240.

15 ### Rockville

County Seat of Montgomery (formerly part of Frederick) County, made the County Seat in 1776. Created a Town by Act of Assembly, 1801. Site of Hungerford Tavern where in 1774, Resolution of Sympathy for Boston was adopted and severance of trade with Great Britain was recommended.   (1)

Site of Hungerford Tavern, in front of Court House.

16 ### Rockville

General J.E.B. Stuart's Confederate Cavalry occupied Rockville June 28, 1863, and captured 150 U.S. wagons along the Washington Road. From here they marched to Gettysburg. In July, 1864, General Jubal

Early passed through Rockville on his way to and from Washington.   (7)

MD 355, south of MD 28, Rockville.

17 ### Rockville
Originally Called Williamsburgh

J.E.B. Stuart and his Cavalry on June 28, 1863 entered here on his famous raid. 900 mules and 150 U.S. wagons were captured near Washington and taken along towards Westminster, Maryland.   (1)

I-270 in median, Rockville.

18 ### Rowser's Ford

This crossing of the Potomac River was used by Confederate General J.E.B. Stuart on the night of June 27, 1863, to enter Maryland on his ride around the Union Army during the Gettysburg Campaign.   (7)

MD 190 (River Road) and Seneca Road.

19 ### Silver Spring

Immediately west of this sign were the Francis P. and Montgomery Blair homes. Confederate General Jubal A. Early used these houses for his headquarters during his operations against Washington on July 11 and 12, 1864.   (7)

MD 97 just north of D.C. Line (Georgia Avenue north of Eastern Avenue).

20 ### Sugar Loaf Mountain

So called in 1710 by a Swiss nobleman - Baron Graffenried who ascended it in search of silver mines with Martin Chartier - a remarkable Frenchman, married to a Shawnee Indian wife, who lived near the mouth of the Monocacy River.   (1)

MD 28, north of B&O Railroad Bridge, Dickerson.

21 ### Tridelphia Lake

This reservoir formed by the Brighton Dam across the Patuxent River is a main source of water supply of the Maryland suburbs of the National Capital. It was

built in 1941-44 by the Washington Suburban Sanitory Commission and contains over 6.5 billion gallons.   (4)

Off MD 650, Brighton Dam Road and Clarksville near Howard County line.

22 ### Washington's Farm
519 Acres owned by the first President

Thomas Sprigg, Jr. patented in 1725 as "Woodstock" 1,102 acres here. Inherited in 1782 by Sprigg's three granddaughters, Sophia, Rebecca and Elizabeth. Sophia married John Francis Mercer (late Governor of Maryland, 1801-1803). In 1794, nearly half of the property was conveyed to George Washington to settle a debt owed by Mercer's father. Washington owned this land at his death in 1799.   (5)

MD 28, 2.3 miles south of B&O Railroad Bridge, Dickerson.

23 ### White's Ferry

This important old ferry and ford were used many times during the war between the states by Lee's Army, Jubal Early, J.E.B. Stuart and others as an entrance to Maryland.   (1)

MD 28 and road leading to Martinsburg.

24 ### White's Ford

About 2 miles northwest was White's Ford. This Potomac crossing was used by General R.E. Lee entering Maryland in September, 1862, and Generals J.E.B. Stuart and Jubal A. Early returning in 1862 and 1864 respectively.   (7)

MD 107 and MD 419.

25 ### Woodstock
"Monte Video"

George Washington's farm of 519 acres acquired by him January 13, 1794 and bought in 1806 by Thomas Peter (whose wife was Martha Washington's granddaughter) as part of her share in Washington's Estate.   (1)

MD 28, 2.3 miles south of B & O Railroad Bridge at Dickerson.

THE BELMONT - Built in 1738 by Caleb Dorsey, this splendid Georgian mansion is now owned by the American Chemical Society. The Belmont has been restored and is now a gracious meeting facility. (See page 33, marker 12).

HOWARD COUNTY

① Adam The First

The first large land grant in what is now Howard County. Patented October 1, 1687 to Adam Shipley who came to Maryland from England in 1668. This marks a section of the Western Boundary of the 500 acre grant. A Shipley Family Cemetery is located among the trees to the east of this marker.   (4)

MD 108, between U.S. 29 and MD 175.

② Bollman Iron Truss Bridge
1869

Spanning the Little Patuxent River is the sole surviving example of the bridging system invented, 1850, by Wendel Bollman, Baltimore Engineer. It was the first system, entirely of iron, used by the Baltimore and Ohio Railroad and the first in America. Through 1873 the company built about 100 such bridges.   (17)

U.S. 1, north of Gorman Road, Savage.

③ Charles Carroll of Carrollton
1737 - 1832

Last survivor of the signers of the Declaration of Independence lived here on his ancestral estate Doughoregan Manor, containing 13,361 1/2 acres originally patented to his grandfather Charles Carroll in 1702.   (1)

U.S. 40 at entrance gate to Doughoregan Manor.

④ Christ Episcopal Church "Old Brick" 1711

Original log Chapel of Ease, Queen Anne's Parish. Erected on "New Year's Gift", a present from the proprietary to Edward Dorsey and Charles Carroll. Improved and made Queen Caroline Parish Church, 1728. First rector, James Macgill. Served 1730-1776. Present building erected 1808.   (4)

Oakland Mill Road, 5 miles north of Snowden River Parkway.

⑤ Cooksville

Site of a skirmish between Confederate Cavalry commanded by General J.E.B. Stuart, and Maryland Militia on June 29, 1863. The Confederates easily defeated their opposition and continued northwardly towards Hood's Mill and Westminster.(7)

MD 97, south of MD 144.

⑥ Dr. Charles Alexander Warfield
1751-1813

The grave of this Revolutionary War Patriot is near this site. A member of the Sons of Liberty, he participated in the burning of the Brig "Peggy Stewart", at Annapolis, October 19, 1774, and also served as a Major in the Elkridge Battalion during the war.   (18)

MD 97, 2 miles south of Cooksville.

⑦ Elkridge Landing

An important Colonial Port for shipment of tobacco. Here in 1765 Zachariah Hood, Maryland's "Stamp Act" agent, was hanged in effigy. Lafayette's Troops camped April 17-19, 1781 on the way to engage Cornwallis in Virginia. George Washington passed many times.   (1)

U.S. 1, south of bridge crossing Patapsco River.

⑧ Ellicott's Upper Mills - 1775

Joseph Ellicott (who with his brothers Andrew and John had established Ellicott's lower mills, now Ellicott City, on the Patapsco River in 1772) built the Upper Mills and his home "Fountaindale" near this spot in 1775. Remaining gravestones of the adjoining family burying grounds were moved in 1974 to the Ellicott Graveyard in Ellicott City.   (19)

Old Fred Road, south of bridge over Patpsco River.

⑨ Friends Meeting House and Graveyard

After founding the town of Ellicotts Mills in 1772 the Ellicott Brothers established this burying ground in 1795 and built the adjacent Friends Meeting House in 1800.   (4)

Old Columbia Pike south of Main Street, Ellicott City.

⑩ The National Road

This marker stands on a part of the right of way of the historic and fabled National, or Cumberland Road. Commencing in 1806 it was built in segments by City, State, Federal and private means and was the first great commercial and travel link from Baltimore to the west.   (20)

MD 144 and Ellicott's Mill Drive, Ellicott City.

⑪ Spurrier's Tavern

Thomas Spurrier's stood at nearby crossroads connecting two important overland routes in colonial days (now U.S. 1 and MD 175). George Washington stopped at least 25 times between 1789 and 1798. His diary noted July 18, 1795: "Dined and lodged at Spurrier's where my sick horse died." Waterloo Inn later occupied the site, but this "popular resort" did not survive into the 20th century.   (5)

U.S. 1, north of MD 175, on grounds of Waterloo Barracks of State Police.

⑫ St. John's Episcopal Church

A Chapel of Ease of Queen Caroline Parish, established 1728. Incorporated by Maryland General Assembly, 1822. Consecrated 1823 by Bishop James Kemp. Original land, "Dorsey's Heaven", deeded to church by Caleb and Elizabeth Dorsey. Present church built 1860.   (4)

MD 144, (Frederick Road), west of St. John's Lane.

⑬ Trinity On The Pike
(Episcopal)

Consecrated by Bishop Whittingham March 26, 1857, as Chapel of Ease for Christ Church, Queen Caroline Parish. Protestant Episcopal Convention approved separation from Christ Church in 1866. Trinity Parish admitted by Convention two years later. Bell Tower added, 1867. Original frame building faced the road. Modified by stone extension, 1890. Rectory rebuilt in 1873 after a fire.   (4)

7474 Washington Boulevard, Elkridge.

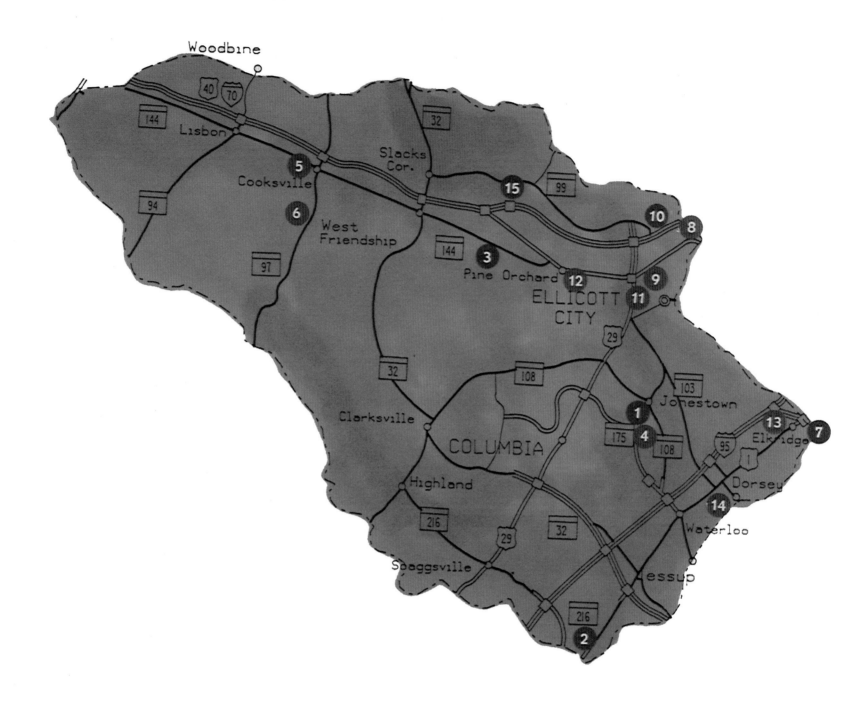

HOWARD COUNTY

Howard County is located southwest of Baltimore City and northeast of Montgomery County and Washington, D.C. In the past it was perceived as a rural & farming community, but has changed into a sophisticated suburban county with the development of the modern city of Columbia.

14. Trinity White Oak

(Seedling in 1768) Prayer of Dedication

O glorious God, whose perfect beauty the wonderful design of all thy work proclaim, bless, we beseech thee, this beautiful old white oak, which we now name "The Trinity Oak" and accept as your gracious gift to this land in remembrance of your mighty power which extends throughout all creation: and we ask that you continue to beautify this place of sanctuary with your presence so that everything that abides here will show forth thy glory, through Jesus Christ, our Lord.   (21)

U.S. 1 between Waterloo and Dorsey Roads.

15. Waverly

The forested land was patented in 1726 by Daniel Carroll of Upper Marlboro, who called it "The Mistake". Earliest part of house was built c. 1760 by Nathan and Sophia Dorsey. In 1786 Edward Dorsey sold 650 acres, including "The Mistake", to Colonel John Eager Howard, Revolutionary Hero and later Governor. When his son, George Howard, married Prudence Gough Ridgely of "Hampton" in 1811, "The Mistake", then totaling 1,313 acres, became a wedding present to the couple. They changed the name to "Waverly" after a popular 1814 novel by Sir Walter Scott.   (12)

Marriottsville Road, north of exit on I-70.

ELKRIDGE FURNACE INN - It is hard to believe that this was once the site of a thriving port for the shipment of tobacco. It was later the site of an iron furnace. It is now a quiet, wonderful inn saved by the Wecker family just before it was to be destroyed.
(See page 33, marker 7).

HAMPTON MANSION - This was once the center of a huge estate stretching for miles both east and west and almost all the way to Pennsylvania. Saved from destruction by the Mellon family, this mansion has been restored and is both a Maryland historic treasure and a national historic site. (See page 39, marker 26).

BALTIMORE COUNTY

1 ### The Baltimore and Harford Turnpike Company

Authorized by the Maryland Legislature in 1816 to open a road from Baltimore City with two branches, one through "Belle Air" to the Susquehanna at Rock Run, and the other to Susquehanna Bridge at McCall's Ferry, Pennsylvania. (1)

MD 147 at Long Green Pike.

2 ### Baltimore County Courthouse

Separation of Baltimore City and County effective July 4, 1851. Townsontown was chosen as County Seat by popular vote February 13, 1854. The Courthouse of local limestone and marble was completed in 1855 at a cost of $30,000. Enlarged in 1910-1925-1958. (4)

Chesapeake Avenue between Baltimore Avenue and Washington Avenue.

3 ### Battle Acre

September 12, 1814

Here General Stricker's City Brigade inflicted severe losses upon the main body of the British Army. This spirited defense together with that of Fort McHenry the next night saved Baltimore. (4)

MD 20, east of Kimberly Road.

4 ### Benjamin Banneker

1731 - 1806

The self-educated Negro mathematician and astronomer was born, lived his entire life and died near here. He assisted in surveying the District of Columbia, 1791, and published the first Maryland Almanac, 1792. Thomas Jefferson recognized his achievements. (4)

Westchester Avenue, west of Oella Avenue, near MD 144, west of Catonsville.

5 ### Brooklandwood Plantation

1798

Built by Charles Carroll of Carrollton for his daughter, Mary Caton. Site of the first Maryland Hunt Cup and Grand National Races. Owned successively by John Cockey, Charles Carroll, George Brown, Captain Isaac Emerson and Saint Paul's School (established 1849). (4)

MD 25 at the entrance to St. Paul School.

6 ### Castle Thunder

A gift from Charles Carroll of Carrollton, Castle Thunder, the home of Richard and Mary Carroll Caton, stood on this site from 1787 to 1906. The 7- mile Frederick Turnpike Stone Marker of 1804 was moved here from its original position 3/10 mile west. (4)

MD 144, west of Beaumont Avenue, Catonsville.

7 ### Clynmalira

5,000 Acres

Surveyed April, 1705, for Charles Carroll, Lord Baltimore's Attorney-General of his Province of Maryland 1688. In 1822 Henry Carroll, Great-Great Grandson of Charles Carroll built Clynmalira house. (1)

Carroll Road, north of Glencoe Road.

8 ### The Colored Methodist Protestant St. John's Chapel of Baltimore County

1833

Originally constructed as a log cabin in 1833, St. John's Chapel and land adjacent thereto served the local black community as a house of worship and burying ground. Services had been held in the present chapel since its construction in 1886. The stone parsonage was built around 1833. Declining attendance forced St. John's to close in the early 1960's. But in the 1980's the property, still owned by descendant's of one of the founders, Aquilla Scott, was restored thru involvement of the Ruxton Community. (109)

7538 Bellona Avenue, Ruxton.

9 ### Colonel William Norris

1820- 1896

Chief of the Confederate States Army Signal Corps and Secret Service Bureau, 1862 - 1865. Appointed Commissioner of Prisoner Exchange with rank of Colonel in April, 1865. The Norris Home, "Brookland", stood 2 1/2 miles south of this spot. His grave is located in All Saints Cemetery, 1 mile northeast. (107)

MD 140 and Cockey's Mill Rd., Reisterstown.

10 ### Commodore Joshua Barney

1759- 1818

Born in Baltimore, Barney at an early age moved with his family to a nearby farm on Bear Creek in the Patapsco Neck section of the County. When only 12 he went to sea. In the War for Independence he was commissioned a 2nd Lieutenant on the "Hornet", and had the honor of flying the 1st American Flag displayed in Baltimore. At the end of the war he was Captain of the "Hyder Ally". In the War of 1812 he served as a privateers man and later as Commodore of a flotilla of gunboats in Chesapeake Bay. In 1814 while serving heroically in the defense of Washington he was wounded and captured. He died in Pittsburgh and was buried there. (4)

Wise Avenue at Patapsco High School.

11 ### Dundalk, Maryland

Founded 1894

Approximately 200 yards northwest of this spot an iron foundry, owned by William McShane, was built in 1894. When asked to give a name to the railroad depot serving his new foundry, he chose "Dundalk" in honor of the birthplace of his father, Henry McShane, born in Dundalk, Ireland. The two seaport communities of Dundalk, one in Ireland and one in Maryland, have many other similarities. (106)

Dundalk Avenue and Dunhill Road.

12 ### "The Eagles Nest"

Part of the Valley of Jehosaphat, now Dulaney Valley, patented August 10, 1684. Walter Dulany acquired half, 1747, and remainder, 1767. His lands were confiscated and sold at the end of the Revolutionary War. Thomas Marsh obtained "The Eagles Nest" portion, 1788. It remained in his family until 1964. (4)

MD 146, 0.5 mile north of Dulaney Valley Road

13 ### Ellicotts Mills

Established 1772 by the three Ellicott brothers from Bucks County, Pennsylvania. They opened the road from here to Baltimore. The B&0 Railroad was completed to this point May 20, 1830. (1)

MD 144, east of bridge, Ellicott City.

14 ### Emory Grove

Founded in 1868 for the purpose of promoting the cause of morality and religion by holding camp meetings under the auspices of the Methodist Episcopal Church.

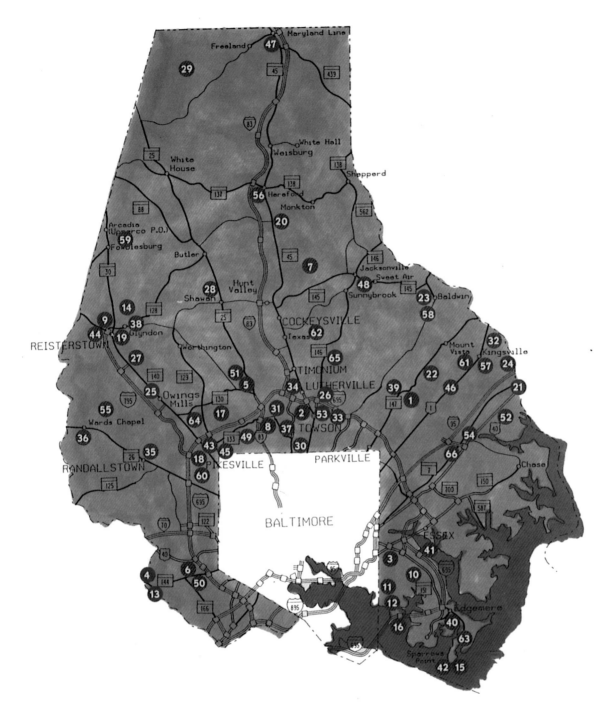

BALTIMORE COUNTY

Baltimore County is a large county extending from Pennsylvania in the north to Anne Arundel County in the south. It completely surrounds Baltimore City. Although Towson, the county seat, has changed from a quiet village to a cosmopolitan, legal, and financial center, the northern section of the county still reflects the rolling farmland of the past. Fox hunting, horse farms, and forests predominate most of northern Baltimore County.

Incorporated 1871 and reincorporated 1884 und present name of the Emory Grove Association Baltimore City. (1
MD 128 and Waugh Avenue.

⑮ Fort Howard
The Bulldog at Baltimore Gate

Built here in 1896 to defend Baltimore from pos ble naval attack. Named for Colonel John Ea Howard, Revolutionary Hero. Five coastal artille batteries bore names of local War of 1812 figur Lt. Levi Claggett; Col. Davis Harris; Francis Sc Key; Judge Joseph H. Nicholson; Brig. Gen. Jo Strickler. A sixth battery honored Dr. Jesse Lazear of Baltimore who gave his life in 1900 to f ther Yellow Fever research. Fort remained und army command until 1940 but its guns were ne fired in anger. (1
Fort Howard Waterfront Park, at end of MD 20.

⑯ Francis Scott Key Memorial Bridge

To the northwest, across the Patapsco, is F McHenry, which British Naval Forces bombard September 13-14, 1814. Detained on a cartel bo Francis Scott Key saw through a spyglass that t star-spangled banner yet waved in the dawn's ea light on September 14 and he was inspired to wr the National Anthem. Some historians placed Ke position about 200 yards west of here. Others say t boat anchored about 3 miles to the southeast. (1
East end of Francis Scott Key Memorial Bridge, Soller Point, I-695.

⑰ The Garrison Fort

Built about 1695 as headquarters for a troop mounted rangers to patrol paths from the Pataps to the Susquehanna as a protection against host Indians. It was nine miles from nearest wh inhabitants when built.
Garrison Farm Court, east of Garrison Farm Roa 0.5 mile north of I-695.

⑱ Garrison Forest Church
(St. Thomas Parish)

A frontier parish church authorized by Act Assembly 1742 as "a Chapel of Ease for the Fore Inhabitants" of Saint Paul's Parish (Baltimor Reverend Thomas Craddock inducted as fi minister January 14, 1745.
U.S. 140, south of St. Thomas Lane.

⑲ Glyndon

By 1860 the Western Maryland Railroad reach

this site. In 1871 Dr. Charles A. Leas employed Augustus Bouldin, surveyor, to plan the town. The railroad and ideal climate encouraged the early development as a resort center with Victorian summer homes, boarding houses, and campgrounds. Glyndon has now become primarily a residential community. (108)

MD 128 and Central Avenue.

 **Gorsuch Tavern**

At "19 mile stone" on York Road built in 1810 by Captain Joshua Gorsuch, a shipbuilder. The tavern was the meeting place of the Baltimore Countians who went to Pennsylvania to reclaim their slaves, thus bringing on the Christiana Riot of 1851. (100)

MD 45, north of Upper Glencoe Road, near Glencoe.

21 Great Gunpowder Falls

Iron enterprises began 1753 by the Nottingham Iron Works and later known as Ridgely's Forges. Then Henry Howard Forges stood over a century on the southwest side of Gunpowder Falls upstream from Route 7. Ruins of Patterson Iron Works built 1820 downstream north shore near the Baltimore and Ohio Railroad tracks. Opposite this mill was a prosperous nail factory (4)

MD 7 bridge over Gunpowder Falls.

22 Gunpowder Copper Works
1804-1883

Levi Hollingsworth built a mill here to roll and fabricate refined blocks of copper that were shipped to Baltimore from Wales and hauled to the mill by ox cart. The copper used for the roofing of the original dome of the Capitol was rolled and fabricated here. (4)

MD 147, 0.2 mile north of Factory Road.

23 Gunpowder Manor
Long Green Valley

In this valley 7031 acres laid out, 1683, for Charles, Third Lord Baltimore. Opened to settlers, 1721, by Charles, Fifth Lord Baltimore. Frederick, Sixth Lord Baltimore, ordered manor sold, 1766. Land remaining 1782 seized and sold as confiscated British property. (4)

Long Green Pike, north of Patterson Road, near Baldwin.

24 Gunpowder River
So Called as Early as 1600

Legend relates that the name originated with an Indian attempt to plant gun-powder in the hope that a crop could be raised. Big Gunpowder Falls flows through Baltimore County, joins the Little Gunpowder Falls at Day's Island to form Gunpowder River. The River empties into the Chesapeake Bay at Carroll Island. (4)

Gunpowder State Park off Graces Quarter Road near bath house.

25 Gwynnbrook State Farm #1

290 Acres, purchased from Dolfield Estate October 29, 1919, from Hunter's License Fund for the purpose of breeding game in captivity for propagation purposes. (3)

Gwynnbrook Avenue and Bonita Avenue, Owings Mills.

26 Hampton
1783-1790 Baltimore County

Estate of the Ridgeley Family from 1745 to 1948. Home of Charles Carnan Ridgely, Governor of Maryland, 1816-1819. One of the largest Georgian Houses in the United States. Now a National Historic Site. (4)

Hampton Lane, east of Dulaney Valley Road, MD 146.

27 Hannah More Academy
Founded 1831

Oldest Episcopal Boarding School for girls in the United States. Mrs. Ann Van Bibber Neilson gave three acres of land at this location and $10,000 to found an academy for girls. The academy became the Diocesan School for the Episcopal Diocese of Maryland in 1873 (4)

U.S. 140 at Caraway Road, near Reisterstown.

28 Hayfields

Colonel Nicholas Merryman Bosley, builder, 1810, awarded Silver Tankard "by the hand of Lafayette" for best cultivated Maryland Farm, 1824. Also home of John Merryman, early importer, 1848, of registered Hereford Cattle, still, 1967, bred here. His imprisonment, 1861, led to Chief Justice Taney's masterful "Ex-Parte Merryman." (4)

Shawan Road, west of Western Run Road.

29 Hoffman Paper Mills

The first paper maker in Maryland was William Hoffman. In 1775 he built his first mill on Gunpowder Falls a quarter mile upstream from the present Hoffmanville Bridge. In September 1776 Congress adopted watermarked paper for its currency. Hoffmanville Mills manufactured this type paper as well as writing and wrapping paper. (100)

Gunpowder Road, North Alesia Road.

30 The Home of Governor Augustus W. Bradford

Which stood on this site was burned July 11, 1864 by Confederate Troops "to retaliate the burning of Governor Letcher's Home" in Virginia by Federal Troops. This was the closest point to Baltimore reached during the war by Confederate Troops. (1)

MD 139, north of Baltimore City Line.

 Hunt's Church
A Methodist Society Established in 1773

First meeting house built on this site 1780. Previously met in Phineas Hunt's House, still standing on Joppa Road. His grave is nearby. The present church building was erected in 1874. (100)

Joppa Road, north of Old Court Road.

32 Ishmael Day's House

When one of Harry Gilmor's Confederate Cavalrymen (on July 11, 1864) pulled down his Union Flag, Day shot him and then escaped to the woods. They burned his house and barn. (1)

Sunshine Avenue, 1 mile east of MD 147, near Kingsville.

 The Joppa Road

Originally an Indian trail used in 1695 by a Troop of Rangers from the Garrison Fort to keep back the Indians. Later the high road to Joppa Town, the County Seat of Baltimore County from 1712 to 1768 and the rival of Baltimore. (1)

Joppa Road, west of Edgecliff Road.

34 Lutherville Historic District
National Register of Historic Places
U.S. Department of the Interior, 1972

Lutherville, named for Martin Luther, was

FOX HUNT - Much of North Baltimore County, above Towson and stretching over into Harford County, is the setting for fox hunts in the fall. Numerous clubs still conduct these hunts on thousands and thousands of acres of fertile farmland. Some of these farms have been owned by the same families for hundreds of years. (See page 37, markers 7 and 12; page 41, marker 38; and page 43, marker 65).

founded, 1852, by Dr. John G. Morris, a Lutheran Clergyman, as the location of Lutherville Female Seminary. The planned village, centering around the Lutheran Church and Seminary, was surveyed into 118 lots by William Sides, 1854. "Oak Grove", 1852, the home of Dr. Morris, one tenth mile east, is a notable example of 19th century architecture. (4)

Front Avenue, south of Morris Avenue.

35 Mt. Paran Presbyterian Church and Cemetery

Paran Church was incorporated September 18, 1841. The church was called Soldier's Delight prior to 1841 and that congregation began circa 1776. The oldest legible tombstone is that of Robert Gilchrist, dated October 17, 1767. The oldest known deed mentions this area as the Plains of Paran, used as a place of worship and burial by the Society of Christians called Presbyterians, dated May 4, 1784. (4)

10308 Liberty Road, Randallstown.

36 New Tavern

Built in 1802 by Robert Ward, the tavern served traffic to and from the west. This was an early Methodist preaching place until 1845. Woodstock Seminarians held Catholic Services here in 1876 for Chrome Mine workers of Soldiers Delight. Holdbrook Post Office was located on the grounds in 1893. (105)

MD 26, east of Wards Chapel Road.

37 Nicholas Ruxton Moore
1736-1816

He commanded "Baltimore Light Dragoons" during the Revolution, attaining rank of Captain. He took active part in suppression of Whiskey Rebellion in 1794, and that year he purchased "Bosley's Adventure", a 350 acre farm west of Roland's Run (north of present Lake Roland). Member of State Legislature 1801-1802, he served in Congress 1803-1811 and 1813-1815. As a Lieutenant Colonel at outbreak of War of 1812, he was appointed Commandant of 6th Regiment Cavalry District of Maryland. His grave near Circle and Ruxton Roads is no longer marked. (101)

MD 134, north of Malvern Avenue.

38 Nicholson's Manor

Patented sixth of August 1719 to William Nicholson, gentleman of Anne Arundel County for 4200 acres. Subdivided in 1757 into four equal parts by Byron Philpot, Junior, Corbin Lee, Kinsey Johns and Roger Boyce. (4)

MD 128 and Longnecker Road, 1 mile east of Glyndon.

39 Northampton Furnace

Built in 1759 by Charles Ridgely (the Elder) of Hampton and two sons, the iron foundry operated for 70 years on Spring Branch of Patterson's Run. It furnished cannon and shot for the Revolution as well as other supplies: "300 kettles" were ordered by the Council of Safety July 15, 1776. "Premature discharge" of cannon tested in 1780 killed Captain John Fulford and "dreadfully wounded" others. The furnace stack is now submerged near here in Loch Raven. (5)

MD 146, north of Chapelwood Lane.

40 North Point
September 12, 1814

Following a dawn landing at the tip of North Point, British Forces passed here en route to Baltimore. About four miles further on they encountered American Skirmishers under Major Heath. (4)

North Point Road, north of Lodge Farm Road on Sparrows Point High School.

41 North Point Battlefield

Where on September 12, 1814 the defenders of Baltimore under General John Stricker met the advancing British Army of 7000 under General Robert Ross, who was killed early in the engagement. (1)

MD 20, east of Eleanor Terrace.

42 North Point Beachhead

At 3 a.m. on September 12, 1814, British began landing troops and supplies here from ships anchored in Old Road Bay. By 6:30 a.m., columns formed on Long Log Lane (now Old North Point Road) when bugles sounded at 7 a.m., 4700 British Soldiers, Sailors and Marines set out for Baltimore. That afternoon, their Commander, Major General Robert Ross, was killed and they were met by Americans in the Battle of North Point. In 2 days of fighting, Baltimore withstood

these land forces and the simultaneous naval attack on Fort McHenry. (103)

Ft. Howard VA Hospital grounds end of MD 20.

43 The Old Court Road

Originally an Indian Trail, then used by the Rangers from the Garrison Fort to keep back the Indians. Later used as a road to the Court at Joppa Town, the County Seat of Baltimore County from 1712 to 1768 and the rival of Baltimore. (1)

U.S. 140, north of Old Court Road.

44 Oldest High School
in Baltimore County

Franklin Academy founded January 10, 1820 by an Act of the General Assembly of Maryland. On January 25, 1849 became a public school. Was Reisterstown High School from 1874-1896. Became Franklin High School in 1897. (100)

Cockeys Mill Road, west of U.S. 140.

45 The Old United States Arsenal

Built in 1816 after the close of the War of 1812 as an arsenal. Removed to a point of safety beyond Baltimore. Used during the War between the States and later as a Confederate Home. Now the property of the State of Maryland. (1)

MD 140, north of Sudbrook Lane, Pikesville.

46 Perry Hall
"The Adventure" 100 Acres

One of the largest houses in Maryland. Begun in 1773 by Corbin Lee. Completed in 1776 by Harry Dorsey Gough. East wing of the Mansion partially burned in 1824. Repaired by Harry Dorsey Gough Carroll circa 1826. Restored by the owners in 1967. (4)

U.S. 1, south of Perry Hall Road.

47 The President, Managers and Company
Of the Baltimore and York Town Turnpike Road

The official title of the Company authorized by the Legislature in 1805 to rebuild and operate the road laid out over this route in 1787 by the State. Made a part of the Maryland Road System 1910. (1)

Baltimore and Yorktown Turnpike at MD Line.

JERICHO COVERED BRIDGE - This is the last remaining covered bridge in Baltimore County. This bridge (Circa 1864) reflects the rural charm of Baltimore County. Located in Kingsville, across the Little Gunpowder Falls River, the bridge is still in use today.
(See page 39, markers 21, 22, 23, and 24 for more information on the area.)

48   **"Quinn"**

500 acre grant in 1704 to Thomas MacNemara. Later called "Sweet Air". Charles and Daniel Carroll, MacNemara's kinsmen, acquired the property and sold it in 1751 to Roger Boyce, who built the present house. It was purchased in 1785 for Henry Hill Carroll, who died here in 1804. His son, Henry Carroll, sold it in 1838.(4)
MD 15, east of Manor Road.

49   **Rockland**

The first inhabitant of this village, dating back to 1706, was Richard Gist, father of the Revolutionary War Hero, Mordecai Gist. The industrial development of the Jones Falls Valley, marked by the building of the Falls Turnpike Road, circa 1806, and later by the Baltimore and Susquehanna Railroad, was the reason for the construction of Rockland Village. Built by the Johnson Family to house the owners of and workers in the Village's various enterprises. The Village also included a blacksmith shop, flour mill, general store and tavern. Through the history of the Village runs the thread of Johnson Family involvement, including three restorations, circa 1880, 1930 and 1983. (110)
Falls and Ruxton Roads, Brooklandville.

50   **Rolling Road**

A Colonial Road built for the purpose of rolling hogsheads of tobacco from the plantations to Elk Ridge Landing for shipment to England. (1)
MD 144, east of MD 166.

51   **Saters Church**
1742

On land granted by the Fifth Lord Baltimore, Henry Sater, gentleman planter, founded this first church of Baptists in Maryland. To the congregation he deeded a plot and chapel "forever to the end of the world." (4)
Corner of MD 25 and Saters Lane.

52   **"Scholars Plains"**
First Free School in Baltimore County

Although a school was built here as early as 1725, by Act of General Assembly this land was sold in 1857. The proceeds were used to erect two schools, one for white, one for colored children, on Philadelphia Road. (100)
Allender Road, north of B&O Bridge between MD 7 and Pulaski Highway.

53 ## Site of Epsom Chapel

Built in 1839 and located just west of this marker on land donated by Henry B. Chew of Epsom Estate. The Chapel served Towsontown both as church and community center. The Chapel was first used by Methodists and became the cradle of Methodism in Towson. Demolished 1950. (4)

East side of Entrance Road to Towson Plaza Shopping Center off Joppa Road.

54 ## Site of Red Lion Inn

An early inn on the Old Post Road at which George Washington stopped many times on his trips between Mt. Vernon and Philadelphia (4)

Red Lion Road, east of Ebenezer Road.

55 ## Soldiers Delight

Chrome was first discovered in the United States in Baltimore County circa 1808. Isaac Tyson, Jr. operated chromite mines at Soldiers Delight and in other serpentine barrens and from 1828 to 1850 his mines produced almost all the world's chronium. The unique beauty of this area is enhanced by rare plants and animals. (100)

Deer Park Road, 0.5 mile south of Wards Chapel Road.

56 ## St. Jame's My Lady Manor

Established 1750 as a Chapel of Ease in the Parish of St. John's of Joppa. In a brick chapel 60 by 30 feet, now the transept, was finished on this site "in the fork of the Gunpowder River" at the cost of 790 pounds. In 1770 by Act of the Maryland Assembly the separate Parish of St. Jame's was established. In 1950 St. Jame's completed two centuries of continuous service. (1)

Monkton Road, west of Old York Road.

57 ## St. John's Parish

(Gunpowder) Established 1692

The old church here standing was built by Edward Day at his own expense and consecrated in 1817 to replace Saint John's at Joppa Town which, built in 1725, lay in ruins. (100)

U.S. 1, north of Bradshaw Road, Kingsville.

58 ## St. John the Evangelist Catholic Church

First Roman Catholic Church in (present) Baltimore County founded in 1822. One and one half miles southeast of Sweet Air, one half mile northeast of Manor Road. Building destroyed by fire February 25, 1855. Parish relocated to present site. First Mass offered December 30, 1855. (4)

Long Green Pike, 0.5 mile north of Hydes Rd.

59 ## St. Paul's Lutheran Church

Believed to be the oldest existing Lutheran Congregation in Baltimore County. It was begun as a Union Church in the early 1700's. The reformed congregation worshiping in the same building. The first recorded communion was in 1794. The first house of worship, built of logs, held about 50 people. The present brick church was built in 1882, with additions in 1892 and 1963. (100)

North side of Dover Road, east of MD 30.

60 ## Sudbrook Park

Rural summer resort designed by Frederick Law Olmsted in 1891 on 20 acres of James Howard McHenry's Estate, "Sudbrook". Minimum lot size was one acre, with limit of one house, one family, two cows and four horses on each. Western Maryland Railway provided 9 trains a day to and from Baltimore. Not surviving are original swimming pool, 9-hole golf course, stables and hotel (which burned in 1926). This triangular lot, "Cliveden Green", was set aside in Olmstead's plan for a church or other public building. (104)

Upland Road, in small triangular lot at east west of Cliveden Road.

61 ## "The Sweathouse Road"

Called for a branch of that name on which the Indians practiced a form of "Turkish Bath" by heating stones in their wigwams and pouring water on them to generate steam which they used as a curative measure. (1)

U.S. 1 and Mt. Vista Road, Kingsville.

62 ## Third and Last County Almshouse

Building constructed and furnished at cost of $60,000 from proceeds of sale of old Almshouse property under authority of County Commissioners granted by Acts of Maryland General Assembly, April 1, 1872. Site purchased from John Galoway. Structure erected in 1872 of stone quarried on premises. Partly destroyed by fire January 1, 1919, promptly remodeled, and fireproofed. Discontinued as Almshouse August 28, 1958. (100)

Van Buren Lane, north of Jefferson Avenue.

63 ## Todd's Inheritance

(National Register of Historic Places)

Thomas Todd settled here from Gloucester County, Virginia, in 1664. Homestead has remained in Todd Family for more than three centuries. Farm once contained 1,700 acres. 17th Century brick house was burned by British Soldiers September 14, 1814, as they withdrew from unsuccessful assault on Baltimore. Rebuilt on site in 1816. Remodeled in 1867. (102)

North Point Road at Avenue C.

64 ## Trentham

Named for free school of Trentham, Staffordshire, England, where Reverend Thomas Craddock had taught. When he married High Sheriff John Risteau's daughter, this estate was her dowry. They built a house in 1746 and in 1747 he opened a boy's boarding school there. The original house, damaged by fire in 1857, was rebuilt in 1860. The octagonal bathhouse dates from 1747. (100)

Cradock Lane, 0.5 mile north of U.S. 140.

65 ## The Valley of Jehosophat

Patented to Richard Smith, Jr. 10th August 1684 for 2500 acres. Daniel Dulaney acquired 1250 acres of this tract 19th November 1724, after which it was called "Dulaney's Valley". (1)

MD 146, north of Timonium Road.

66 ## "Whitemarsh"

Rochambeau's Troops camped here September 11, 1781 where the baggage train and heavy artillery rejoined them. After the victory at Yorktown the French Troops, in five divisions, camped here again on their way northward, at the end of August 1782. (4)

Ebenezer Road, northwest of U.S. 40.

Mount Clare Mansion

Davidge Hall

B&O Railroad Museum

Fells Point

MOUNT CLARE MANSION - is Baltimore City's oldest colonial mansion and was built in 1754.
The **B & O RAILROAD MUSEUM** and the Mount Clare Mansion are related by the railroad tracks which run between them.
Reenactments of the Civil War and other periods are staged throughout the year when they are both open to the public.
DAVIDGE HALL is the oldest structure in the country in continuous use as a medical school. **FELLS POINT** was established in 1726 by William Fell, a shipbuilder from England. This area retains much of its early charm.

BALTIMORE CITY

❶ Bon Secours Hospital

Congregation of the Sisters of Bon Secours, a nursing order founded in France in 1824, sent three sisters to Baltimore in May 1881, at the request of Cardinal Gibbons. Their first U.S. Convent opened at West Baltimore and Payson Streets the following year. The Sisters were soon widely known for their untiring and compassionate care of the sick. Bon Secours Hospital began here with 22 beds in 1919. Marker erected in 1981 to celebrate 100 years of health care on this site. (4)
2000 West Baltimore Street

❷ The Canton Library

The Enoch Pratt Free Library (Branch #4) was one of the four branches given to the City. Begun in 1883 and opened for use in 1886, this is the only original branch still in use as a library. The library is a pleasant and interesting building in the victorian style. Designed by Charles Carson, it has been altered very little over the years. The Canton Library owed its existence to the famous Baltimore philanthropist, Enoch Pratt. Prior to its construction, Enoch Pratt worked in a reading room one block to the south. This location, Ellwood Avenue and Elliott Street was the site of the Reading Room where Enoch Pratt worked with the Welsh and other immigrant groups to teach them the values and pleasures of reading. Pratt became so involved with this purpose that he was led to believe that this free library concept should be a part of his town, Baltimore. It was thought by many that Pratt considered this Canton library his pet project. He followed every phase of its construction from the cornerstone to the joyous completion. (87)
1030 South Ellwood Avenue.

❸ Clover Hill
(so named circa 1714)

Part of "Merryman's Lott." 210 acres of virgin timberland granted by Lord Baltimore in 1688 to Charles Merryman, whose descendents farmed here until 1869. Stone house built in 19th Century occupied by

Bishops of Maryland since 1909, when cathedral site purchased by Episcopal Diocese. Charles Carroll of Carrollton, signer of Declaration of Independence, acquired portion south of Merryman's Lane (now University Parkway) for access to Homewood circa 1801. (4)
University Parkway, east of Charles Street.

❹ Davidge Hall

Davidge Hall, constructed in 1812, is named for the first dean of the University of Maryland School of Medicine, Dr. John B. Davidge. Noted for its unique classical appearance, it is the oldest building in the country used continuously for medical education. The Medical School, established in 1807 by the Maryland General Assembly was the fifth to be founded in the United States. Following mergers with Baltimore Medical College, 1913, and College of Physicians and Surgeons, 1915, the School became part of the State University System in 1920. (4)
Lombard Street, east of Green Street.

❺ Enoch Pratt Mansion

Built, 1847, by Enoch Pratt (1808-1896), merchant and philanthropist, who generously presented the City of Baltimore with the Enoch Pratt Free Library, and was a liberal benefactor to many other institutions. Purchased, 1916, by Mrs. H. Irvine Keyser, who renovated and enlarged it and presented it to the Maryland Historical Society, 1919, as a memorial to her husband. The building now contains Francis Scott Key's original manuscript of "The Star-Spangled Banner", the Library of the Society, and period rooms. (4)
201 West Monument Street.

❻ Evergreen On The Falls
(National Register of Historic Places)

Surveyed for John Walsh in 1754. Large square cupola once crowned brick mansion, built in Italianate style c. 1860 by Henry

Snyder. Leased after 1864 to James Hooper, owner of Meadow Mill. Estate was sold in 1870 to David Carroll, co-owner Mount Vernon Mills. Acquired by Maryland Society for Prevention of Cruelty to Animals in 1926. Granite structure, 1860, was valve house for Hampden Reservoir (filled with earth from Jones Falls Expressway excavation .) (4)
Falls Road (MD 25), north of I-83 south ramp.

❼ Federal Hill

Since the founding of Baltimore, 1729, this hill has been a popular point for viewing the City's growth. Here 4,000 people feasted, 1788, to celebrate the ratification by Maryland of the Federal Constitution and in honor of the new government gave the place its name. An observatory built here 1795, signaled city merchants of the approach of their vessels, a service which lasted a century. Shipyards have long been located near the hill, and it has been mined for clay and sand. During the Civil War, Union Troops fortified the site, and it was made a public park, 1880. (4)
South side of Key Highway, Inner Harbor.

❽ Fells Point

A colonial maritime community established 1726 by William Fell, shipbuilder of Lancashire, England. In this area were built more than six hundred ships from the Colonial era through the Civil War. Birthplace of the U.S. Frigate "Constellation" and home port of the famous Baltimore Clipper. (86)
Broadway, north of Thames Street.

❾ First Boy Scout Armory

On this site, May 20, 1911, Ernest Thompson Seton, founder of the Boy Scouts of America, laid the cornerstone of the first Boy Scout Drill Armory in the United States, and 30 acres of land were presented to the Mount Washington Boy Scouts for park and parade ground purposes. (Commemorative stone given by the Women's Club of Mount

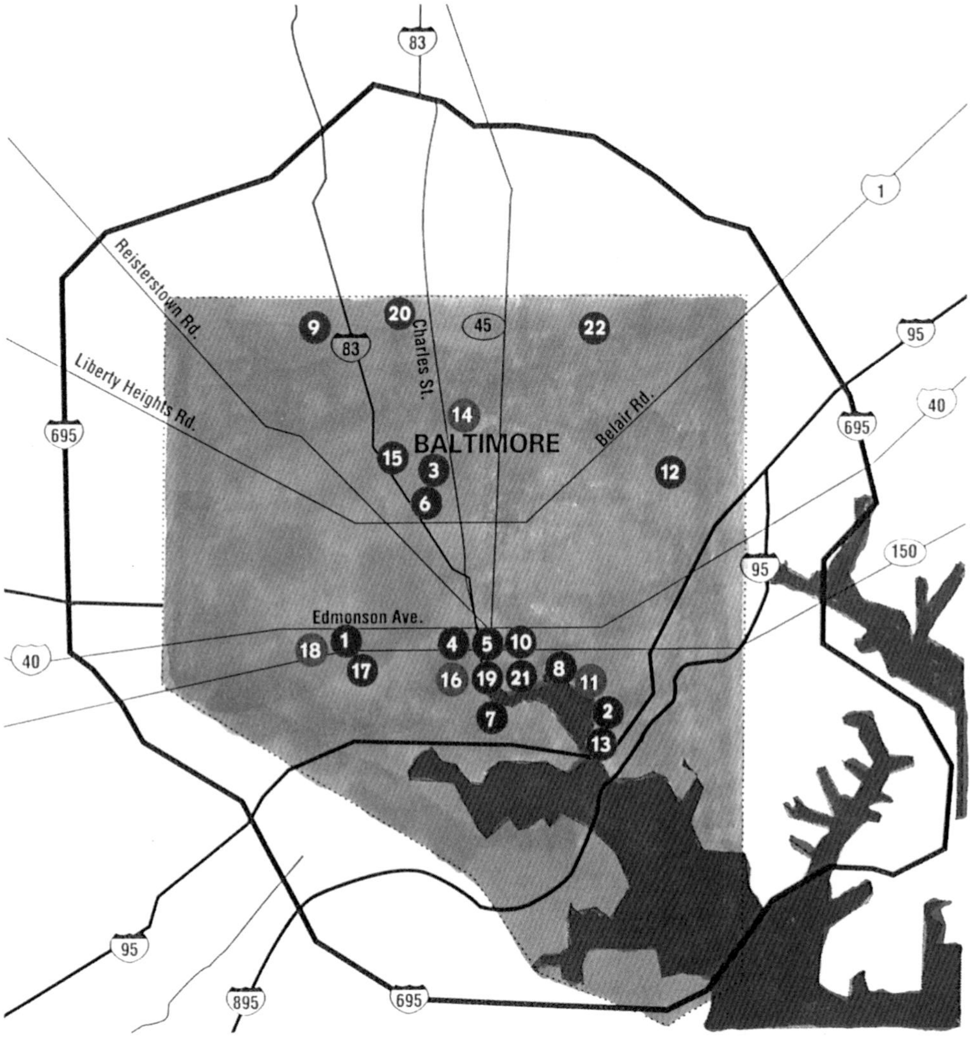

BALTIMORE CITY

Baltimore City is the largest city in the State of Maryland. It is the center of commerce and culture of the state. In recent years it has become a tourist attraction because of its historical significance and the development of the Inner Harbor.

Washington, October 11, 1969.) (4)

Kelly Avenue, east of Bonne View Road and Cross Country Boulevard.

🔟 First Dental College

The Baltimore College of Dental Surgery, first Dental College in the world, chartered by the General Assembly of Maryland March 6, 1840. Founders were Horace H. Hayden, M.D., D.D.S., and Chapin A. Harris, M.D., D.D.S. The Assembly, stipulated by Act of Consolidation April 9, 1924, that the name of the College "shall be preserved as a definite department of the University of Maryland." The name adopted: "Baltimore College of Dental Surgery, Dental School, University of Maryland." Tablet in Hopkins Plaza, six blocks east, marks original site of the College. (85)

666 West Baltimore Street.

1️⃣1️⃣ Frederick Douglass

1817- 1895

Frederick Douglass, when a twelve years old, was sent to serve the Auld family in a home on this site. He secretly taught himself to read and write. After escaping from slavery, he became a renowned orator with an international reputation and the publisher of an Abolitionist newspaper, "The North Star". In 1891, he was appointed United States Minister to Haiti. (4)

Corner of Aliceanna and South Durham Streets

1️⃣2️⃣ Furley Hall

On hill to the north stood the Georgian Mansion built c. 1775 by Daniel Bowley, II (1745-1807), Baltimore merchant and patriot of the Revolution. He was a Town Commissioner, 1771-1778, and three times a State Senator. In 1814, British Soldiers occupied the Estate. It was purchased in 1847 by William Corse, Sr. (1804-1869), whose garden was a favorite of his friends Enoch Pratt and Johns Hopkins. Damaged by fire in 1906. Furley Hall was razed in 1953. (5)

Parkside Drive and Brehms Lane.

1️⃣3️⃣ Historic Canton

Through the efforts of the Canton Improvement Association this old and densely populated ethnic neighborhood was named to the National Register of Historic Places in 1978. The two-story red brick row houses are especially noteworthy for their hand-painted screens, white marble steps and occasional movable wooden steps. Canton's beginnings are steeped in history. The U.S. Frigate Constellation, now in the Inner Harbor, was launched in 1797, at Major Stodder's Shipyard on Harris Creek. The Canton Ironwork rolled the armor plates for the U.S.S. Monitor in the 1860's. The Canton Company was involved in the building of the first American locomotive, the Tom Thumb. The first Whig Convention was held at Canton Race Track in May 4, 1840 when Henry Clay and Daniel Webster spoke and William Henry Harrison was nominated for President. (87)

Corner of Potomac and O'Donnell Streets.

⓮ Homewood

Part of tract surveyed in 1670 for John Homewood. Charles Carroll of Carrollton purchased farm from Thomas Homewood in 1794. Carroll, signer of the Declaration of Independence, built this country house, 1801-1803, as a wedding present for his son, Charles, Jr., who married Harriet Chew of Philadelphia July 17, 1800. House is considered an outstanding example of Federal Architecture. Brick barn with cupola to the south also dates from 1803. (83)

In median of North Charles Street, north of Greenway.

⓯ Keswick

The Home for Incurables of Baltimore City, was incorporated November 1, 1883, through leadership and resources provided by the men and women of the Hospital Relief Association of Maryland. The purpose of this organization, incorporated December 18, 1880 was "to care for and brighten the days of the weary patients in the hospitals of Baltimore City." The former location of the home was 1640 East Fayette Street (1884-1887), and Guilford Avenue and 21st Street (1887-1926) and since 1926

the Home, now known as Keswick, has been at this location. (4)

700 West 40th Street.

⓰ Lexington Market

This world famous market, named for the Battle of Lexington, was established 1782, on land given by Revolutionary War hero, General John Eager Howard. It operated in the open until the first building was erected, 1803. So choice was its food, so phenomenal its growth, that Oliver Wendall Holmes, 1859, declared Baltimore to be "the Gastronomic Metropolis of the Union." During the Revolutionary War French troops under Count De Rochambeau, returning from Yorktown, camped on this ridge then known as Howard's Hill. (4)

Paca Street at Calvert Street, south of Saratoga Street.

⓱ Mount Clare

Baltimore's oldest Colonial mansion, begun 1754. Home of Charles Carroll, Barrister (1723-1783), noted Maryland Patriot and Revolutionary War Statesman. Maintained as a public museum. Opened daily except Monday. (84)

Monroe Street at entrance to Carroll Park.

⓲ Mount Olivet Cemetery

The burial place of Methodist Pioneers including Bishops Francis Asbury, Enoch George, John Emory and Beverly Waugh, also Robert Strawbridge, first preacher in Maryland and Jesse Lee, founder in New England. Site of 1966 Methodist Bicentennial. The capsule to be opened in 2066. (4)

Frederick Avenue (MD 144) west of Fonthill Avenue.

⓳ Rectory of Old St. Paul's Parish

Incorporated 1692, 37 years before Baltimore Town itself, St. Paul's moved to this vicinity in 1731. It was City's first place of public worship. This Rectory, the "Parsonage on the Hill", built 1789-1791 on half-acre lot given by Colonel John Eager Howard, replaced earlier house at present location of Fidelity

Building, Charles and Lexington Streets. The church at Charles and Saratoga Streets, designed by Richard Upjohn in 1854, is fourth on Baltimore's original "Lot 19". (84)

Corner of Cathedral and Saratoga Streets.

⓴ Roland Park

(National Register of Historical Places)

One of Nation's oldest planned garden suburbs, named for Roland Thornberry, a Baltimore County landowner. English investors sacked 100-acre development proposed by William Edmunds and Edward H. Bouton, and the Roland Park Company was incorporated July 30, 1891. Landscape architect George Kessler laid out first plat east of Roland Avenue. In 1897 Frederick Law Olmstead, Jr., took up planning of steepe terrain on the west side. This tudor-style commercial structure pioneered the "shopping center" concept in America. (82)

Roland Avenue, north of Upland Road.

㉑ Site of Poe's Death

This structure, now the East Building of Church Hospital, was erected in 1836, to house the Washington Medical College. Edgar Allen Poe, author and poet, was brought here, ill and semi-conscious, on October 3, 1849 and died four days later. In 1857, the building was purchased by Church Home and Infirmary, which was renamed Church Home and Hospital in 1943. (153)

100 North Broadway.

㉒ Taylor's Chapel

The Taylor family, whose land holdings in area by end of 17th century were extensive, constructed of logs on the site c. 1770 a Quaker Meeting House, later used for Methodist services. It was razed when present stone chapel was built in 1853. Through the years many denominations have worshiped here. Graveyard stones date from 18th century. Earliest part of nearby Taylor Homestead built c. 1764. (81)

On Mt. Pleasant Golf Course off Hillen Road.

LIRIODENDRON MANSION is one of Harford County's hidden treasures in the town of Bel Air. It is named for the tulip trees that surround the house. Originally the house of Dr. Kelly, one of the founding physicians of Johns Hopkins Hospital, it has been restored and is open to the public for weddings, tours and meetings. (See page 49, marker 2).

HARFORD COUNTY

① Aberdeen Proving Ground
Four Miles

Military reservation of 55000 acres of land and water. The Ordinance Department, U.S. Army operates here: the Army Proving Ground for Arms, Ammunition and Automotive Equipment: the Ballistic Research Laboratory: the Ordinance School. Established 1917.   (1)

U.S. 40 and MD 22.

② Bel Air
County Seat of Harford County
Est. 1783

Court House erected 1791. Burned and re-erected 1858. Enlarged 1904. Portraits of notable men born in Harford adorn court room, including Edwin Booth, who gave his first theatrical performance there.   (26)

Main Street (MD 924) between Office Street and Courtland Street.

③ Black Horse Tavern

George Washington stayed here the night of June 5, 1773 on his way back to Mt. Vernon from Columbia College, New York, where he had left his stepson Jackie Custis.   (1)

MD 23 and MD 138.

④ "The Bush Declaration"
Harford Town

County Seat of Harford County from its origin March, 1774, until March, 1783. Here the first Declaration of Independence ever adopted by an organized body of men duly elected by the people was proclaimed on March 22, 1775.   (4)

MD 7 at Bush, 3 miles northeast of MD 24.

⑤ Captain Angus Greme

One of two officers in Lafayette's Army who, according to tradition, were so struck with the view from here that they vowed to return after the Revolution. Greme did settle nearby with his family and in 1850 he was buried beside Trappe Church, then a Chapel of Ease (established 1760) of St. George's Episcopal Parish. Present stone building dates from 1875.   (5)

MD 136 and Trappe Road.

⑥ Captain John Smith

In 1608 ascended this river to this point. On his map he called it after his home in England "Willowbyes Flu" or river. Now Bush River.   (4)

U.S. 40, 0.7 mile west of Otter Point Road.

⑦ Churchville
Formerly called "Lower Cross Roads"

Council of Safety met here 5 April, 1775. Considered as site for county seat 1781. George Washington passed 6 May, 1775 on way to be made Commander-In-Chief of Army. Lafayette and his troops marched past 15 April, 1781 on the way to Virginia. Part of Rochambeau's Troops passed through Sept. 1781 toward Yorktown.   (1)

MD 22 and MD 136.

⑧ Colony of Maryland
1634- 1776

Maryland founded as a Proprietary Colony by Lord Baltimore, March 25, 1634. Religious toleration established by Act of Assembly, 1649. Mason-Dixon Line surveyed 1763-1767. The British Stamp Act repudiated, 1765. "Peggy Stewart" Tea Party, Annapolis, 1773. Maryland signed Declaration of Independence July 3, 1776.   (4)

I-95, Maryland Restaurant Grounds.

⑨ Conowingo

An Indian name meaning "at the falls." Captain John Smith ascended the Susquehanna River in 1608, to the head of tidewater. He named the first rapids "Smiths Falls".   (22)

U.S. 1 at Conowingo Dam.

⑩ "Constant Friendship"
Acquired 1761 by
Colonel Thomas White (1704-1779)

Largest colonial landowner in this part of Maryland. Deputy Surveyor-General of Baltimore (then including Harford) County. Father of Bishop William White, first presiding Bishop of the Episcopal Church and Chaplain of the Continental Congress.   (22)

MD 92, south of Box Hills Parkway.

⑪ "The General's Highway"

This is a section of "The General's Highway" route of General Washington's triumphant journey, December 2-23, 1783, New York to Annapolis, to resign as Commander-in-Chief of the first "American Army".   (24)

U.S. 40 in square at Aberdeen (removed).

⑫ The Governor Nice Highway

(Removed when the name of the highway was changed.)   (l)

U.S. 40 near Pennsylvania Railroad Bridge, at beginning of dual highway near Havre de Grace.

⑬ The Gunpowder Neck

One of the earliest settled sections of the Upper Chesapeake Bay 1658-60. Now the site of U.S. Edgewood (Chemical Warfare) Arsenal and Fort Hoyle.   (1)

Edgewood Road and U.S. 40.

⑭ Hall's Cross Roads

At intersection of Old Post Road (established 1666) and Bush Neck Road (1670) were a tavern and relay point for stagecoaches in 18th Century. In 1835 nearby stop on Philadelphia, Wilmington and Baltimore Railroad was named for Aberdeen, Scotland, birthplace of the first station master. Hall's Cross Roads, Mechanicsville and Aberdeen incorporated as Aberdeen in 1893   (25)

MD 132 (Bel Air Avenue), approximately 0.2 mile south U.S. 40.

⑮ Harford Town or Bush

Count de Rochambeau's Troops bivouacked here September 10, 1881-their 32nd camp on the way to Yorktown. The American Troops had gone in advance.   (1)

U.S. 40.

⑯ Harford Town or Bush

The French Troops of Count de Rochambeau in five divisions camped here at the end of August 1782 - the 22nd camp on the return march from the Yorktown Victory to the north.   (1)

MD 7 at Bush Road.

HARFORD COUNTY

Harford County is located east of Baltimore County in Central Maryland. The county is a combination of suburban, industry, and rural farms among the beautiful rolling hills of the area. The equestrian traditions of Maryland are seen throughout Harford County in horse farms, jousting matches, and fox hunting.

⓱ Harry Gilmor's Raid

On July 10, 1864, Major Harry Gilmor's Confederate Calvary camped in this building (an old stage coach headquarters) on his way to burn the Pennsylvania Railroad Bridge across the Gunpowder, where he captured General W. B. Franklin. (1)
MD 152 and Old Joppa Road.

⓲ Havre de Grace

Here on the morning of May 3, 1813, British Forces under Admiral Cockburn landed, sacked, and burned the town. The principal defenses were two small batteries on Concord Point. The "Potato Battery" on high ground, was manned to the last by John O'Neill. (4)
Concord Street, north of Lafayette Street.

⓳ The Hays House

Circa 1711

A dwelling of the type owned by a family of moderate means, soon after the frontier reached this area. Occupied by seven generations of the Hays-Jacobs Family. Moved from its original site in 1960 by the Historical Society of Harford County and now its headquarters. (4)
MD 924, east of U.S. 1 business, Bel Air.

⓴ "Indian Spring"

Count de Rochambeau's Heavy Artillery and Baggage Train camped near this point September 10, 1781. After fording the Susquehanna River at Bald Friar they proceeded to Bush to join the main troops. (1)
MD 136, 3.4 miles north of MD 22.

㉑ Jerusalem Mills

Established 1772 by David Lee a Quaker from Bucks County, Pennsylvania. A gun manufactory back of the mill furnished guns for the Revolution in 1776. The original tract called Jerusalem patented 1687. (1)
Jerusalem Road north of Little Gunpowder Road.

㉒ Joppa Town

2 miles

County Seat of Baltimore County from 1712 to 1768. Once a rival of Baltimore, an important point for shipping tobacco and a Port of Entry. Benjamin Rumsey, First Chief Judge of the Court of Appeals, lived here. (4)
U.S. 40, west of Joppa Farm Road.

23 Ladew Topiary Gardens and Pleasant Valley House

Henry Scarff acquired land here about 1747 and soon built a four-room house. Descendants added the three story central section by 1849. Harvey S. Ladew bought the house and property known as Pleasant Valley Farm from a Scarff descendant in 1929. Ladew added wings and a portico, greatly enlarging the house. He designed and planted magnificent topiary gardens that are now known world wide, and collected rare plant material with which to furnish his imaginative series of garden rooms. (4)

MD 146, 1 mile south of MD 152.

24 Lafayette

And his troops camped April 13, 1781, one mile north of this point at Colonel's Rigbie's House, after fording the Susquehanna at Bald Friar, on his way to engage Cornwallis at Yorktown. Part of Rochambeau's Troops also passed over this route on their way to Yorktown in August, 1781. (22)

MD 440 and Castleton Road.

25 Lafayette
At Colonel Rigbie's House

Had Lafayette failed in quelling the mutiny of his troops here on Friday, April 13, 1781, the Battle of Yorktown might never have been fought. (22)

MD 623, 0.7 mile north of U.S. 1.

26 Medical Hall
Two miles north of this point

Birthplace and home of Dr. John Archer, 1741-1810. First graduate of medicine in America, signer of the Bush Declaration March 22, 1775. Member of Congress 1802. One of the founders of the Medical and Chirurgical Faculty of Maryland. Father of five physicians. (22)

Corner of MD 22 and Thomas Run Road.

27 Mason-Dixon Line
40th Mile Stone

Maryland-Pennsylvania boundary line surveyed and marked 1763-68 by two English Astronomers, Charles Mason and Jeremiah Dixon. This is one of the "Crown" stones, set every five miles displaying the Coat of Arms of Lord Baltimore on south and the Penns on north sides. Intermediate miles marked by stones with M facing Maryland and P facing Pennsylvania. Stones imported from England. (1)

MD 23 on MD-PA Line.

28 My Lady's Manor
"Lord Baltemore's Guift"

10,000 acres patented September 10, 1713, to Margaret "Lady Baltemore, Baroness of Baltemore" fourth wife of Charles, Third Lord Baltimore and bequeathed by her in 1731 to his Lordship's Granddaughter Charlotte (Calvert) Brerewood. (1)

MD 16, 0.5 mile south of Pocock Run

29 Old Post Road
Established 1666

Count Rochambeau's Troops camped here September 9, 1781 after having crossed the Susquehanna River on their way to the Siege of Yorktown, Va. (23)

MD 7 and Old Bay Lane, Havre de Grace.

30 Old Post Road
Established 1666 Cokesbury College

First Methodist College in world established at Abingdon June 5, 1785 by Bishop Thomas Coke and Francis Asbury. Destroyed by December 4, 1795. Located 175 yards east of this point. (23)

MD 7, 2 miles east of MD 24, at its intersection with Colesbury Road.

31 Old Post Road
Established 1666
Gov. William Paca

Signer of the Declaration of Independence. Born October 31, 1740 on Chilberry Hall Farm, 1 1/4 miles south of here. Died October 27, 1799. (23)

MD 7, 0.4 mile north of MD 24

32 Old Post Road
Established 1666
Harford Town

County seat of Harford County from its origin March 1774 until March 1783. Here the first Declaration of Independence ever adopted by an organized body of men duly elected by the people was proclaimed on March 22, 1775. (23)

At Bush, on MD 7.

33 Old Post Road
Established 1666
Joppa Town

Located on the Gunpowder River two miles south of this point. County Seat of Baltimore County 1712 to 1768. A great tobacco market and Port of Entry prior to the Revolutionary War. (23)

U.S. 40 and Joppa Farm Road.

34 Old Post Road
Established 1666
Spesutia P. E. Church

Founded in 1671. First church erected at Gravelly near Michaelsville. The three succeeding churches erected on the present location. One mile south of this point, colonial vestry house erected 1766. (23)

MD 7 and MD 159, one mile west of Aberdeen.

35 Old Post Road
Established 1666
Susquehanna Lower Ferry

Public Ferry ordered established by the Council of Maryland 1695 for travel between north and south. General Washington and many notable men used this ferry, also, the Continental Army and soldiers of war between the States. (23)

MD 7A (Union Avenue) and St. Johns Street, Havre de Grace.

36 "Olney"

Surveyed as "prospect ye 29th August 1705 for Thomas Preston." Named changed to "Olney" in 1810 by Mrs. John Norris, an admirer of Cowper, the poet, and his friend, the Reverend John Newton, who lived at Olney, England. (1)

Old Joppa Road, 0.5 mile east of MD 152.

37 Peach Bottom Slate Region

Peach Bottom Slate, first used 1734, is the

51

Ladew Topiary Gardens

Ladew Main House

Ladew Library - Main House

LADEW TOPIARY GARDENS - was acquired by Harvey Ladew in 1929. He greatly expanded the house and added what would become a world class topiary garden. His magnificent European style, humor and love of horses and fox hunting can be seen through the house and gardens.
(See page 51, marker 23).

oldest in America. The first commercial cut having been made 1785 by workmen who were primarily Welsh. At the London Crystal Palace Exposition, 1850, Peach Bottom Slate was judged best in the world.   (4)

MD 165 and MD 136 near Whiteford.

38 **Rochambeau Plaza**

Named for the French General whose Troops passed through here in 1781 en route to Yorktown. Records of the French Army noted plans were underway for a Town at this place when the Troops returned from Yorktown in 1782.   (156)

St. John and Washington Streets, Havre de Grace.

39 **Rock Run**

Rock Run House, the home of Brigadier James J. Archer, who resigned from the United States Army to join the Confederacy. Wounded and captured at Gettysburg July 1, 1863, General Archer died in Richmond October 24, 1864. shortly after his exchange.   (7)

On grounds of Rock Run State Park.

40 **Rock Run Landing**

Part of "Land of Promise" tract. Original mill (1760), present grist mill (1794), first Susquehanna River Bridge (1818) and Barge Canal (1839) made through this hamlet a thriving commercial center. Surviving are Miller's House, the Mill, Toll House and Owner's Mansion (1804). Remains of canal and bridge piers are also visible.   (27)

Rock Run and Stafford Roads.

41 **St. Ignatius Church**

Hickory, Maryland

Oldest Roman Catholic Church in continuous use in the Archdiocese of Baltimore. Completed in 1792 by Sylvester Boarman, S.J., while in charge of the nearby Jesuit Mansion of St. Joseph at Priest's Ford. Early pastors of the church served Charles Carroll of Carrollton and his neighbors in the Chapel at Doughoregan Manor, Howard County. St. Ignatius is the mother church of six others in Baltimore, Cecil, and Harford Counties.   (4)

U.S. 1 and Old Jarrettsville Road.

42 **Site of "Old Baltimore"**

The first County Seat of Baltimore County, 1659 to 1700, was located on Bush River. In 1683 it was made a Port of Entry by the Maryland Assembly.   (1)

At head of Bush River on U.S. 40.

43 **Site of Old Baltimore**

circa 1670

Here beside Bush River was County Seat of Baltimore County, then largely wilderness including what is now Harford County. By 1676 Courthouse has been built, about 1/4 mile south of surviving cemetery of Phillips Family. (Here is buried Martha Paca Phillips, sister of William Paca, signer of Declaration of Independence.) In 1683 Maryland Assembly made this village a Port of Entry for Trans-Atlantic vessels. By 1693 Court had moved west to "Simm's Choice" on Gunpowder River, relocating again in 1712 at what is now Joppatowne. Present Baltimore City on the Patapsco was founded in 1729.   (28)

Waterfront on Bush River at Chibury Point, Old Baltimore Road (restricted area of Aberdeen Proving Ground).

44 **Sophia's Dairy**

(probably Sophia's Dowry)

Left by Captain Hall of Cranberry in 1737 to his daughter Sophia, who married Colonel Thomas White, father of Bishop William White of Philadelphia, Mrs. Robert Morris and Sophia, who married Aquilla Hall. He built this house in 1768, one of the finest colonial buildings in Harford County.   (1)

U.S. 40 at Belcamp Industrial Park.

45 **Spesutia Church**

St. George's Parish Episcopal

Founded in 1671 at Gravelly, where original wooden structure no longer stands (about 2 miles southeast, on Aberdeen Proving Ground). Parish moved here in 1718. Present church, erected in 1851, is third on this site. Brick Vestry House here dates from 1766. Early graves were moved from Gravelly. The name Spesutia is derived from the Latin for Utie's Hope, 17th century Manorial Grant to Colonel Nathaniel Utie.   (28)

MD 159, west of Spesutia Road.

46 **Spesutia Island**

(Utie's Hope - 2300 Acres)

Surveyed 1658 for Nathaniel Utie member of Governor's Council. Erected into a manor 1661. Treaty of Peace with Chiefs of Susquehannough Indians signed here May 1661 by Governor Phillip Calvert and Council. (1)

U.S. 40 in square at Aberdeen. (removed)

47 **Spesutia Island**

The name is derived from the Latin for Utie's Hope. A 2,300 acre Manorial Grant in 1661 to Colonel Nathaniel Utie, for whom this island was surveyed in 1658. Settling here from Virginia, Utie traded with the Indians, became a member of the Maryland Governor's Council and represented Lord Baltimore in a boundary dispute with the Dutch in Delaware. A peace treaty with the Susquehannoughs was signed on the Island by Governor Philip Calvert and his council May 16, 1661. A house built by Utie at this end of the island no longer stands.   (12)

Spesutia Island Road, west of Island.

48 **State of Maryland**

1776 - 1964

General Washington resigned his commission at Annapolis, December 23, 1783. American Revolution officially ended by Congress meeting in Annapolis, January 14, 1783. District of Columbia given to Nation, 1791. Francis Scott Key wrote "The Star Spangled Banner", Baltimore, September, 1814. Nation's first national highway, railroad, and telegraph established in Maryland.   (4)

I-95, Maryland Restaurant Grounds.

49 **Tudor Hall**

The home of the noted actor Junius Brutus Booth, the elder. Birthplace of his children. His son Edwin Booth was born here November 13, 1833.   (22)

MD 22, 3 miles south of Bel Air at entrance to Tudor Hall.

50 **William Paca**

Signer of the Declaration of Independence. Born at Chilbury Hall, Harford County, 1740. Died and is buried at Wye, 1799. Governor of Maryland 1782-85.   (1)

MD 7, 0.6 mile east of MD 24.

ST. MARY ANNE'S CHURCH - is one of the oldest buildings in Cecil County. Built in 1742 in the town of North East. The "Bible" and "The Book of Common Prayer" presented by Queen Anne of England in 1718 to the church, are still in use for special services. (See page 61, marker 55).

CECIL COUNTY

1 ### The Anchorage

Home of the Lusby's in the early 1700's. Ruth Lusby and Commodore Jacob Jones married in 1821, made the Anchorage their home and enlarged it in 1835. Jones served on the "Philadelphia" when it ran aground at Tripoli and Commanded the Sloop "Wasp" during the War of 1812. (4)

MD 213, 0.5 mile north of MD 282.

2 ### Bald Friar Ford and Ferry

Near Pilot, two and one-half miles Northwest of this point, lies the site of a Susquehanna fording used by Indians before the coming of the white man. By 1695 a barge provided ferry service to the Colonists. The Conowingo Lake now covers the site. On April 12, 1781, Lafayette moved his troops South by way of the ford, followed by Rochambeau's artillery and baggage detachments on September 10 of the same year. (38)

Corner of U.S. 222 and Oakwood Road

3 ### Blue Ball Tavern

Established about 1710 on lot no. 35 of "the Nottingham Lots" by Andrew Job who secured it from William Penn. Job's son, Thomas, married Elizabeth Maxwell, niece of Daniel Defoe who wrote "Robinson Crusoe." (4)

MD 273 and Blue Ball Road

4 ### Bohemia
Formerly Milligan Hall

Home of George Milligan (1720-1783), Scotch Trader. Purchased from his son, Robert, by Louis McLane (1784-1857), who represented Delaware in the United States House and Senate, was Minister to Great Britain, Secretary of Treasury, Secretary of State, and President of the Baltimore and Ohio Railroad (not open to the public.) (4)

MD 213, 0.8 mile south of Bohemia River.

5 ### "Bohemia Manor"

Granted 1662 as 4000 acres in the "Farr Remote, then unknown wilderness" to Augustine Herman, native of Bohemia, for "making a map of this province". Regranted 1663 as 6000 acres. Erected a manor in 1676.

Not open to the public. (1)
MD 213, 0.8 mile north of Bohemia River

6 ### Brick Meeting House

William Penn set aside lot no. 30 (500 acres) of the "Nottingham Lots" in 1702 for a "common" and site of a "meeting house" as a bold move in the boundary line dispute with Lord Baltimore. It has been continuously used since the first log meeting house was erected in 1709. (1)

Brick Meeting House Road, west of MD 272.

7 ### Brookland

Land Grant by Lord Baltimore, 1732 to present log wing, believed built in 1735. George Gale added fieldstone section circa 1781. Further additions to house were made in 19th Century. Gale, born in Somerset County in 1756, served in Continental Army during Revolutionary War, was member of Maryland Convention which ratified Federal Constitution (1788) and was elected to first U.S. Congress (1789). He died here in 1815, is buried nearby at St. Mark's Church. (36)

St. Marks Church Road, 0.3 mile west of U.S. 222, Perryville.

8 ### Calvert Village

40-acre Grant from William Penn in 1701 on which present East Nottingham Friends Meeting House built, 1724, with stone addition completed in 1752. Used as American Army Hospital in 1778. Cross Keys Tavern, built in 1744, was midway on Old Baltimore-to-Philadelphia Pike. Village known as "East Nottingham," "brick meeting house house" and "the brick" before Post Office adopted present name in 1878. Lafayette's Army camped in woods here April 12, 1781. White oak at old crossroads ring-dated by Maryland Forestry Service to circa 1661. (39)

MD 273 and Rosebank Road, west of MD 272.

9 ### Captain Michael Rudulph

During Revolutionary War this daring officer commanded Cecil County Troop of Lee's Legion, the Cavalry of Lieutenant Colonel Henry (Lighthorse Harry) Lee. Near here in 1778 Rudulph is said to have led squad

disguised as poultry peddlers who boarded and captured British Man-of-War blockading the Port of Charlestown. His cousin, Major John (Fighting Jack) Rudulph also served with distinction in Lee's Legion. (33)

Water Street, Charlestown.

10 ### Charlestown

Laid out and erected as a town by Act of Assembly in 1742 "there being as yet no such place settled at, or near, the head of Chesapeake Bay." George Washington records many visits to Charlestown in his diary. He lodged here August 10, 1795 and September 9, 1795. (1)

Market and Bladen Streets, Charlestown.

11 ### Cherry Grove

Ancestral home of the De Veazie (Veazey) family, patented to John Veazey circa 1670. His descendant, Colonel Thomas Ward Veazey, defended Duffy's Fort, Fredericktown, from the British fleet May 5, 1813, and served as Governor of Maryland, 1836-1839. He is buried here in the family graveyard with his three wives. Not open to the public. (4)

Cherry Grove Road, 9 mile west of Stoney Battery Road, south of Bohemia River.

12 ### Colonel Nathaniel Ramsay

Member of Council of Safety and Courageous Officer of the Maryland Line in Revolutionary War, native of Pennsylvania, Princeton Graduate, (1767) and lawyer. He settled in brick house near this site after his marriage in 1771 to Margaret Jean Peale. In 1775 he and his Brother-in-law, famed portrait painter and inventor Charles Wilson Peale, conducted experiments here in manufacturing of gunpowder. Serving under Washington in 1778, Ramsay was wounded at Monmouth, New Jersey, and taken prisoner by the British. After the war he served 2 terms in Congress. (5)

Market and Bladen Streets, Charlestown.

13 ### Count de Rochambeau's Troops

Crossed the Susquehanna River in five divisions and made their 23rd camp here at the end of August 1782 on the return from Yorktown Victory to the North. (1)

Perryville near Rogers Tavern.

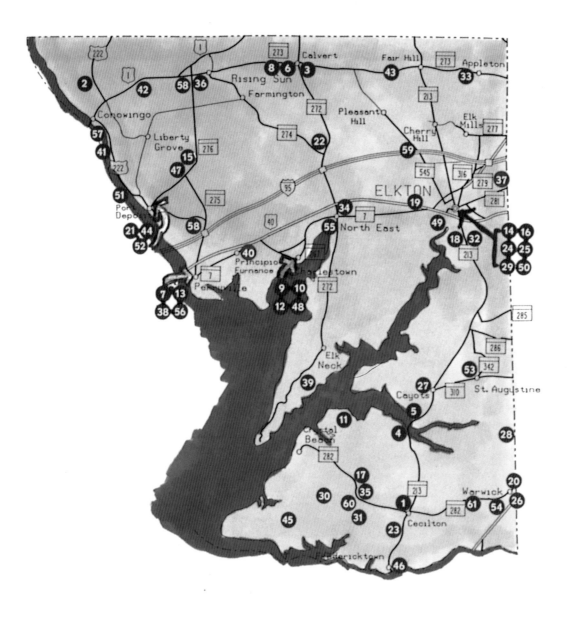

CECIL COUNTY

Cecil County is at the very top of the Chesapeake Bay. Geographically it has one "foot" in Central Maryland and the other in the Eastern Shore. It is predominately farmland, but the Bay and rivers offer excellent hunting, fishing, and boating.

14   Creswell Hall

The home of John A. J. Creswell who nominated James Buchanan for president in 1856 and turned Republican in 1861. He was successively Assistant-Adjutant General of Maryland, member of the House of Representatives, Senator and Postmaster by appointment by President Grant.   (7)

MD 7, approximately 0.3 mile east of MD 281, Elkton.

15   Cummings Tavern

Count de Rochambeau's heavy artillery and baggage train camped here September 9, 1781 before fording the Susquehanna at Bald Friar and proceeding to join the main Army on the Philadelphia Road.   (1)

MD 276, north of Dr. Jack Road.

16   Elkton

Originally called "Head of Elk"

Lafayette embarked his troops March 8, 1781 to capture Benedict Arnold. Returned April 9, began overland march to Virginia April 12, 1781. Washington and Rochambeau with their combined forces stopped September 6-7, 1781 on way to Yorktown.   (1)

MD 268 and MD 7, Elkton Town Hall.

17   Essex Lodge

Granted to Samuel Brocus, whose daughter Susannah married, circa 1700, Edward Veazey. Their son, Colonel John Veazey, Sr., was Chief Military Officer of Cecil County and Justice and Judge for 22 years. His eldest son, Edward, was High Sheriff of Cecil County, 1752-1753; his fourth son, Dr. Thomas Brocus Veazey, inherited from him Essex Lodge and married the daughter of Reverend William Thompson, Rector of St. Stephen's Church. Not open to the public.   (4)

Glebe Road near Earleville.

18   Frenchtown

Frenchtown, one mile west of this marker, was an important link in the North-South travel route during the 18th and 19th Centuries. As a depot, it was burned by the British under Admiral Cockburn on April 29, 1813.   (4)

MD 213 and Frenchtown Road.

19 *This is a section of*
"The General's Highway"

This is a section of "The General's Highway". Route of General Washington's triumphant journey, December 3-23, 1783, New York to Annapolis, to resign as Commander-In Chief of the First "American Army". (31)

U.S. 40, east of MD 279.

20 ## George Washington

Visited Warwick February, 1756, March 1756. "Din'd and lodg'd at Mr. D. L. Heath's" May 1773. Passed through September 3 and October 28, 1774. Breakfasted March 23, 1791 and again in September 1793. (1)

MD 282, 0.1 mile west of Church Road.

21 ## Gerry House

Built 1813, probably by Daniel Megredy. Lafayette was entertained here in 1824. Later owned by Cornelius Smith (1792-1858), farmer and philanthropist who financed road construction to create jobs for the unemployed and aided public education in Port Deposit. Smith willed house in 1858 to his stepgrandson, Lucius A. C. Gerry, who saw action in the Civil War as artillery officer in Captain Alonzo Snow's Battery B. (35)

U.S. 222, south of MD 276, Port Deposit.

22 ## Gilpin's Falls Covered Bridge

Built circa 1860, the bridge is one of the few covered ones left in Maryland and the only one on public ground in Cecil County. The area to the East has been the site of several mills, the earliest Samuel Gilpin's Flour Mill circa 1735. Bridge restored 1959 through the joint effort of the State Roads Commission and the Historical Society of Cecil County, led by Fletcher P. Williams, Past President. (4)

MD 272, 3 miles north of U.S. 40.

23 ## Greenfield

Georgian Manor House, built in the mid 1700's on a 750 acre tract patented to John and Mary Ward in 1674. Is noted for it's architectural purity, fine paneling and woodwork. The Ward burying ground nearby also contains graves of Lusbys and

Pascaults, later owners. Greenfield is listed in the National Register of Historic Places. (32)

MD 213, 1 mile south of MD 282 .

24 ## The Hermitage

Port of Friendship tract and home of Robert Alexander, Delegate to Provincial Convention 1774 and to Continental Convention 1776. August 25, 1777 he hosted Washington here and 3 days later offered allegiance to British General Howe. Devoted to loyalist cause, he left his wife and lived in London until his death. His estate, which included most of the present town of Elkton, was confiscated and sold, but his wife retained this house. (40)

323 Hermitage Drive, Elkton.

25 ## Holly Hill

Built circa 1810-1820 by James Sewall. He was Clerk of Cecil County Court, 1805-1841; Brigade Major of Maryland Militia and a Commander at nearby Fort Defiance in War of 1812; one of founders of Trinity Episcopal Church, Elkton in 1832. (34)

MD 213 and entrance to Big Elk Mall.

26 ## James Rumsey

The inventor of the steam boat was born 1743 two miles north of this point in "Middle Neck". George Washington showed much interest in Rumsey's experiments and made him Superintendent of "The Potomac Company". (1)

MD 282 and Sandy Branch Road, Warwick.

27 ## "Labadie Tract"
Comprising 3750 Acres

Obtained in 1684 from Augustine Herman by the religious sect called Labadists. Here they led an austere form of Communistic life but disintegrated about 1698. (1)

MD 213 and MD 310.

28 ## Little Bohemia
in Middleneck

Owned originally, 1726, by Joshua George from Queen's County, Ireland, who was an attorney and surveyor general for the Eastern Shore. His son, Sidney George, Sr., represented Cecil County in the Maryland

General Assembly 1751. The latter's son, Sidney George, Jr., was justice of the Peace and his great-grandson, Henry Banning Bradford was long identified with the house. Not open to the public. (4)

Telegraph Road and Middlesex Road.

29 ## Mitchell House

Built in 1769 as the home of Dr. Abraham Mitchell, noted physician. During the Revolutionary War he converted the house into a hospital for the use of wounded soldiers of the Continental Army. General Lafayette was a friend of the Mitchell family and visited here. (32)

East Main Street, Elkton.

30 ## Mount Harmon Plantation
Tobacco Prize House and Wharf

Originally owned by Godfrey Harmon, then by James Paul Heath; subsequent to 1760 the home of James Louttit, Sr. and Jr., and Sidney George, Jr., Patriots. Vestry men on St. Stephen's Church, and contributors, 1782, to the original endowment of Washington College, Chestertown, Maryland. (4)

Grove Neck Road, 1 mile west of Pond Neck Road, near Earleville.

31 ## Mount Pleasant

Built by Dr. John Thompson Veazey, 1825, "of Mount Harmon" as he was known, who, with Colonel Thomas Ward Veazey assisted in the defense of Duffy's Fort, 1813. He was a greatnephew of George Ross, signer of the Declaration of Independence. His son, Thomas Brocus Veasey, was captured and shot by Cubans during the Lopez Expedition, 1851. Not open to the public. (4)

Grove Neck Road, 1 mile west of Sandy Bottom Road, near Earlville.

32 ## New Castle and Frenchtown Railroad
1832-1853

One of the earliest in the United States. The line ran from New Castle on the Delaware River, crossed the highway here, and extended to Frenchtown on the Elk River

TURKEY POINT LIGHTHOUSE - is close to the site that on August 25, 1777, Sir William Howe landed 15,000 British troops. Coming from New York in a fleet of some 300 ships the troops proceeded toward Philadelphia, along the Elk River, where they engaged and defeated Washington at Brandywine.
(See page 59, marker 39).

$1^1/_2$ miles west of this point. (4)

MD 213 and Lewis Shore Road.

33 "New Munster"

A tract of 6,000 acres laid out in 1683 by George Talbot (then Surveyor General of Maryland) for Edwin O'Dwire and 15 other Irishmen. Its northern boundary extended into what is now the state of Pennsylvania. (1)

North side of MD 273, west of Big Elk Creek Bridge.

34 North East

George Talbot of Susquehanna Manor renamed North East River, "The River Shannon". The iron forges of the Principio Company were located here. Saint Mary Ann's Parish Church is one of the oldest in Cecil County. Russell one of the owners of the Principio Company, lived nearby. (4)

MD 7, west of North East.

35 North Sassafras Parish
(Episcopal)

Established by Act of Assembly in 1692. The first vestry met January 10, 1693 in the Court House at Ordinary Point. The Parish Church was "dedicated to the honor of Saint Stephen", March 25, 1706. Rebuilt 1737, 1823 and 1873. (4)

MD 282 Spur and Glebe Road, Earleville.

36 The Nottingham Lots

37 Lots of approximately 500 acres each given by William Penn to his colonists in 1702 although they lay in Maryland and were part of George Talbot's "Susquehanna Manor" of 32,000 acres granted him in 1680 by Lord Baltimore. (1)

MD 273 one mile east of Rising Sun.

37 The Old "Post Road"
Established 1666

When it crosses the Mason and Dixon line, dividing the States of Maryland and Delaware. (29)

Where it crosses the Maryland-Delaware Line, on MD 281.

38 The Old Post Road
Established 1666
Lower Susquehanna Ferry
Established 1695

Roger's Tavern where George Washington frequently stopped between 1781-1798. (29)

MD 7, just prior to entrance to V.A. Hospital grounds.

39 Overlook of General Howe's Landing

On August 25, 1777, after a month's voyage from New York, 15,000 British troops led by Sir William Howe disembarked on the shores of the Elk River approximately 2 miles east of this site. The fleet of 300 vessels which had transported them was under command of the General's brother, Admiral Richard Howe. Heavy thunderstorms subsided the night of August 27 when the British began their cautious march toward Philadelphia along both sides of the Elk. On September 11, they engaged and defeated Washington's army in the Battle of Brandywine. (37)

Turkey Point Road, south of MD 272.

40 The Principio Company

The first iron works in Maryland erected about 1715 by British Iron Masters. Augustine Washington (the father of George) owned one-twelfth interest in the company. (1)

MD 7 at Principio Furnace.

41 The Proprietors of the Susquehanna Canal

The corporate title of the company authorized in 1783 to build one of the first inland waterways in America. The bed of this canal and some of its stone locks are still visible near this road. (1)

U.S. 222, 3 miles south of U.S. 1.

42 Richards Oak

General Lafayette and his Army camped around this tree April 12, 1781. A Civil War Cavalry Unit later occupied the site. The Oak, over 500 years old, was owned by the Thomas Richards Family for over a century. A huge limb fell August, 1964, splitting the trunk. In 1965 the tree measured 85' in height, 24' in girth and 115' in spread. Tree preserved 1922-1960 by Hytheham Club, Port Deposit. Restored 1965 by Historical Society of Cecil County. (4)

U.S. 1 and Love Run Road.

43 Rock Presbyterian Church

Founded 1720 in North Milford Hundred, Cecil County, Maryland. First called New Erection on the Branches of Elk River, then Elk River Church, Great Elk, Upper Elk and, since 1793, Rock. Present Church erected 1761; remodeled in 1844 and 1900. (4)

MD 273 and Rock Church Road.

44 Rock Run Mill

Built circa 1725. Owned by John Steel, this great mill was in successful operation as early as 1731. At the same period a ferry was operated about one half mile downstream at a crossing known as Upper Ferry. (4)

U.S. 222 and Granite Avenue, Port Deposit.

45 Rose Hill

Home of General Thomas Marsh Forman (1758-1845), Aide to General William Alexander, know as Lord Stirling, and a representative in the General Assembly, 1790 and 1800. He served with Major George Armistead, Fort McHenry, 1814. A later owner, William Ward, represented Cecil County in the General Assembly, 1875, and married Charlotte Ringgold Knight of Essex Lodge. Not open to the public. (4)

Grove Neck Road, 1.3 miles west of Pond Neck Road, near Earleville.

46 Sassafras River

Discovered and explored by Captain John Smith 1607-1609 who named it Tockwough River after the tribe of Indians who inhabited its banks. Tockwough was the original Indian name for Sassafras, a root from which they made a form of bread. (30)

Fredericktown end of Sassafras River Bridge (plaque).

47 Site of Chapel-of-Ease

To St. Mary Anne's Church, North Elk

Rodgers Tavern

North East

Gilpin's Falls Covered Bridge

GILPIN'S FALLS COVERED BRIDGE - was built circa 1860. The bridge was restored in 1959.
RODGERS TAVERN - Built near the lower Susquehannah Ferry in 1695. George Washington frequently stopped here between 1781 and 1798. **NORTH EAST** - seems to be surrounded and focused on water. There is fishing and waterfowl almost everywhere. (See page 57, marker 22; page 59, markers 34 and 38).

Parish, North East, Maryland. Built in 1733. The oldest remaining gravestone in 1968 records the death of Thomas Shepherd, August 28, 1742. (4)

Near Woodlawn north side of Dr. Jack Road, 0.3 mile west of MD 276.

48 Site of Charlestown Wharf

Stone wharf and warehouse were built here by Decree of General Assembly in 1744. Remains of wharf can be seen. Officer's chests left behind by two Companies of Royal American Regiment quartered in winter of 1756-1757 were auctioned by town commissioners circa 1759. During Revolutionary War this as major supply depot for American Armies. In 1813 British Troops destroyed earthworks built to guard wharf and town. (33)

Colonial Wharf Park, Conestoga and Water Streets, Charlestown.

49 Site of Fort Defiance

About one eighth mile Southeast on Elk River. American forces here and at Fort Hollinsworth (Elk Landing) repulsed the British under Admiral Cockburn in their attempt to capture Elkton, April 29, 1813. (4)

Oldfield Point Road, north of Jones Chapel Road.

50 Site of Fort Hollingsworth

About three tenths mile south at Elk Landing. American forces here and at Fort Defiance, about one mile below on Elk River, repulsed the British under Admiral Cockburn in their attempt to capture Elkton, April 29, 1813. (4)

Landing Lane and Oldfield Point Road, Elkton.

51 Smith's Falls

In 1608 Captain John Smith ascended the Susquehanna River until stopped by the rocks. On his map he calls this point "Smyths Fales" marking it by a + which he explains as meaning "Hath bin discovered what beyond is by relation." (1)

U.S. 222, 0.5 mile north of MD 269.

52 Snow's Battery

On August 30, 1861, Battery B of the Union Army, under the Command of Captain Alo-nzo Snow, was organized at Port Deposit. Composed mainly of men from this town and vicinity, the Battery rendered important service to the Federal Forces in the Civil War. Notably artillery support in two bloody battles of 1862; Malvern Hill, on the James River in Virginia, and Antietam, near Sharpsburg in Maryland. (35)

U.S. 222 south of MD 276, Port Deposit.

53 St. Augustine's Church

First called "Mannour Chappel" a Chapel of Ease of North Sassafras Parish. Established in Bohemia Manor in compliance with an Act of the Maryland Assembly, 1692. Erected as a separate Parish in 1744. (4)

MD 310 and MD 342.

54 St. Francis Xavier Church
"Old Bohemia" - 2 miles

Founded 1704 by Reverend Thomas Mansell, S.J. One of the earliest permanent Catholic establishments in the English Colonies. Bohemia Academy founded 1745 by Reverend Thomas Pulton, S. J. attended by Charles Carroll of Carrollton, a signer of the Declaration of Independence, and his cousin, John Carroll, first Catholic Bishop in the United States. (4)

MD 282 and Church Road.

55 St. Mary Anne's Church
North Elk Parish-1706

The building, erected 1742, is one of the oldest in Cecil County. The cornerstone bears the initials of the Rector and Vestrymen at that time. Communion vessels, a bible and a book of common prayer presented 1718 by Queen Anne of England still are used for special services. (4)

MD 272 in North East between Church and Thomas Streets.

56 Susquehanna Manor

Know also as New Connaught Manor, or New Ireland. This manor of 32,000 acres was one of the largest in Maryland. It was granted, 1680, to George Talbot (a cousin of Charles Calvert, Third Lord Baltimore) of Castle Rooney, Ireland, in return for his promise to bring 640 colonists of Irish and British descent to Maryland. (4)

MD 7, one mile east of Perryville.

57 A Susquehannock Indian Fort

Located at this point was an important factor in the boundary line controversy between Lord Baltimore and William Penn in 1683. (4)

MD 222 between Port Deposit, Conowingo Dam.

58 West Nottingham Academy

Founded 1714 by Samuel Finley, Presbyterian Minister and a native of County Armagh, Ireland. He remained in charge of the Academy and Church until 1761 when he was chosen President of the College of New Jersey, now Princeton University. (4)

2 Markers: One on U.S. 1 cut-off, and one at I-95 exit near Perryville.

59 Wilna

William Whann Mackall was born at Wilna January 18, 1817. Resigning from the U.S. Army, he joined the Confederacy and served on the staffs of Generals Albert Sydney Johnston, Braxton Bragg and Joseph E. Johnston. General Mackall surrendered at Macon, Georgia, April 20, 1865. (7)

MD 545 under I-95 overhead bridge, 2.2 miles north of MD 279.

60 Woodlawn
Formerly "Neighbor's Grudge"

The 305 acre farm of William Ward. He gave a tract called "North Levell" on which stands St. Stephen's Church. His descendent, Henry Veazey Ward, was Consul General for the Republic of Chile. Another, Juliana Veazey Ward, married Dr. George Read Pearce of "Pearce's Neck", grandson of George Read, signer of the Declaration of Independence. Not open to the public. (4)

Grove Neck Road, 0.1 mile east of Pond Neck Road, near Earleville.

61 "Worsell Mannor"
1000 Acres

Patented 5th June, 1685, to Major Petersayer, a prominent Catholic. Later acquired by the Heath Family. On 14th May, 1773, George Washington "Din'd and lodg'd at Mr. D. L. Heath's" taking his stepson Jackie Custis to King's College, New York (Columbia University). Governor Eden accompanied them to Philadelphia to attend the races. (1)

MD 282 and Worsell Manor Road.

WASHINGTON COLLEGE - is one of the oldest colleges in the United States. It was built in 1782 in Chestertown. George Washington granted the use of his name as well as served on its Board of Visitors and Governors. Washington received his Doctors of Law in 1789 from the college.
(See page 64, marker 17).

KENT COUNTY

1 Bass Propagation Lake

Fairlee Mill Pond, Kent County, one mile from this point. Purchased by State 1928.   (2)
MD 20 at Fairlee.

2 Battle of Caulk's Field
War of 1812

Kent County Militia under Lt. Col. Phillip A. Reed marched from Belle Air (Fairlee) to meet British Forces here on August 31, 1814. The British with 15 killed, were repulsed, and their commander, Sir Peter Parker, mortally wounded. American losses were slight.   (4)
MD 20, 0.3 mile north of MD 21.

3 Brig. Gen. John Cadwalader
1742 - 1786

Commander Penna Troops. Served at Princeton, Brandywine, Germantown and Monmouth. Incensed at the cabal against Washington he wounded General Conway in a duel. Lived nearby and served in General Assembly of Maryland from Kent County. Buried in Shrewsbury Churchyard. His epitaph was written by Thomas Paine.   (1)
MD 213, 0.7 mlle south of MD 444.

4 Captain Lambert Wickes

One of senior officers of Continental Navy in opening years of Revolutionary War. Noted for his daring raids on British shipping. In his Sloop of War Reprisal he took Benjamin Franklin to France in 1776. Was first American Naval Officer in European Waters after Declaration of Independence. Born near here on Eastern Neck Island, c. 1735. He was lost with his ship in storm off Newfoundland October 1, 1777. Franklin called him "a gallant officer, and a very worthy man."   (93)
MD 20 and MD 445.

5 Caulk's Field Monument

The British commanded by Sir Peter Parker Baronet and the Americans commanded by Col. Phillip Reed met in engagement on this field August 31st 1814. The British were defeated and Sir Peter Parker killed. Erected A.D. 1902 by Marylanders to commemorate the patriotism and fortitude of the victor and vanquished.   (97)
Caul's Field Road, 0.1 mile west of MD 21.

6 Chestertown, Maryland

County seat of Kent County. Established In 1706. Situated on the most traveled highway between south and north during the Revolutionary Period. George Washington made eight known visits here between 1756 and 1793. Rich in Colonial History.   (96)
High Street, south of Cross Street, Chestertown

7 Colonel Isaac Perkins
Patriot of the Revolution

Son of Thomas Perkins, who built brick house near here in 1720. The Colonel was one of the Commissioners appointed by Maryland Council of Safety to raise supplies for Washington's Army. Much of the flour provided from the Eastern Shore was ground in the mills of his property. In 1780 he accused tory "Villans" of hiring "some abandoned wretch" to set fire to his mills.   (5)
MD 213, 1 mile south of MD 292.

8 Crew's Landing

In 1715 Edward Crew leased Fish Hall (Fishall Patent 1664) for 11 years at the yearly rate of one ear of corn. Crew purchased 60 of the original 225 acres for 3000 Ibs. of tobacco in 1726 and the remaining 165 acres in 1728. Fish Hall later became known as Crew's Landing. It was condemned on April 18, 1866 for a public landing. The County Commissioners paid the Crew Family $78.43.   (99)
MD 292 (Main Street), Betterton

9 Downs' Cross Roads
Galena, Maryland

On this site stood the tavern erected by William Downs in 1763. Burned in 1893. George Washington stopped here in 1774 en route to and from the first Continental Congress. He traveled this road on his eight visits to Kent County.   (94)
MD 213 and MD 29, Galena.

10 Georgetown, Maryland

Erected by Act of Assembly of Maryland, May 1736, on a tract called Tolchester. A base of Continental supplies, 1775 to 1783. Port of Entry and ferry landing. George Washington stopped here en route to points north and south. Burned by British May 6, 1813.   (89)
MD 213, south of the bridge, Cecil County Line.

11 George Vickers

George Vickers was born in Chestertown in 1801. He opposed secession in 1861. Assisted Governor Hicks to raise an Eastern Shore Regiment, and attained the rank of Major General of Militia. In the trial of President Johnson, Senator Vickers voted for acquittal.   (7)
MD 213, north of MD 20.

12 The Kent County Free School

Here stood the Kent County Free School authorized and established by Act of Council and Assembly of Maryland September 26, 1766. This became Washington College October 15, 1783.   (154)
MD 213, north of MD 20.

13 Martin Wagner
1899 - 1980

Master Machinist and Blacksmith, he was the third generation of his family to devote his life to work with forge, torch and anvil on this site. The Wagner Blacksmith and Machinery Repair Shop began serving the residents of Kent County in the 1850s. Besides repairing manufactured equipment, the Wagners created many new products for farmers and watermen. The Wagner skills made life easier for many generations of people covering a wide area of the Upper Eastern Shore.   (95)
MD 20, west of Martin Wagner Road

14 Protestant Episcopal Church

In this church was held the first convention which proposed and adopted the name Protestant Episcopal Church November 9, 1780.   (92)
MD 289 and Park Row #2 on south wall Emmanuel Protestant Episcopal Church.

15 Rock Hall

Formerly known as Rock Hall Cross Roads. Main Street is part of first road cut in Kent County in 1675. George Washington passed

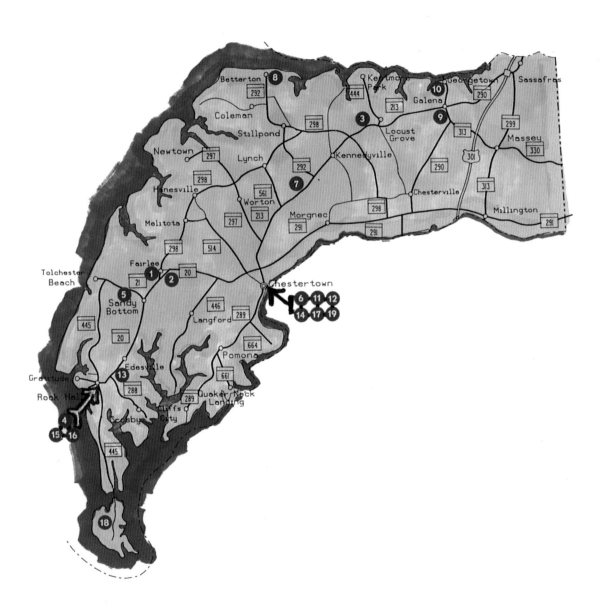

here eight known times. Tench Tilgman used this route from Yorktown to Philadelphia in October 1781. (93)

MD 45 (Main Street) and Sharp Street.

16   Rock Hall Landing

Site of Rock Hall Mansion for which the town was named. Landing of Annapolis - Rock Hall Packet used by George Washington on eight known trips through Kent County. A convenient route used by many prominent persons of Colonial and Revolutionary periods. (93)

Hawthorn Avenue and Sharp Street.

17   Washington College
Founded in 1782

George Washington gave to its founding, granted use of his name and served on the Board of Visitors and Governors. He Attended public exercises here, 1784, and received degree of Doctor of Laws in 1789. (90)

MD 213 on Campus of Washington College.

18   Wickliffe

Major Joseph Wickes, who settled on Eastern Neck Island c. 1658, was Chief Justice of Kent County. Before 1674 the Court met at Wickliffe, his home here (no longer standing). By 1680 he had acquired 864 acres, the southern half of the island, which he held until his death in 1692. His great-grandson Captain Lambert Wickes, who spent his early years here, served with distinction in the Continental Navy, was lost at sea with his Sloop-of-War Reprisal October 1, 1777. (98)

CO 115, north of Parking Area on Eastern Neck Island.

19   Worrell's Tavern

Site of the Tavern where George Washington dined and lodged on his return from Philadelphia, March 23, 1791, while he was President of the United States of America. (1)

MD 289 (Queen Street) and Cannon Street, Chestertown.

KENT COUNTY

Kent County is located just south of Cecil County and is an upper bay area bordered by Delaware to the east and the Chesapeake Bay to the west. It is full of wonderful bay scenics and picturesque farms.

CHESTERTOWN - has been the county seat of Kent County since 1706. Washington stopped here at least eight times during the Revolutionary War because this was on one of the most traveled roads between the north and south. (See page 63, marker 6).

CENTERVILLE COURTHOUSE - is the oldest courthouse in continuous use in the State of Maryland. Built between 1791 and 1796 in what would later become Centerville. In the park, in front of the courthouse, is a statue of Queen Anne which the county is named after. (See page 67, marker 10).

QUEEN ANNE'S COUNTY

① Bennett's Point Farm

Originally called "Morgan's Neck". Surveyed in 1658 for Henry Morgan of the "Isle of Kent" as two tracts of 150 acres each. Henry Morgan was given the land for transporting two indentured servants into the province. The Tracts descended to Morgan's wife Frances in 1663 and to his daughter Frances Sayer, wife of Col. Peter Sayer, in 1676. In 1698, the farm passed to Elizabeth Rousby, granddaughter of Henry Morgan, and wife of Richard Bennett III. It left ownership of Morgan descendants in 1793 when sold to Col. James Hindman. In 1801, it was acquired by Major Richard Tilgman whose heirs owned it until 1871. Richard and Elizabeth Bennett are buried nearby in the partially restored chapel. (59)

Morgan's Neck Road and Bennett's Point Road.

② Birthplace of Charles Willson Peale

First Free School of Queen Anne's County erected near here 1724. Its sixth master was Charles Peale, father of the distinguished portrait painter and museum founder - born 1741 in living quarters near the school. Luther Martin, renowned Barister, was among the school's masters who later attained distinction in public service. The school's visitors were local Colonial Leaders and among the pupils were many of the forefathers of the County's Prominent Citizens. (4)

MD 18 and Wrights Neck Road.

③ "Bloomingdale"

Patented 7 June, 1665, by Captain Robert Morris as "Mount Mill". Purchased by Jacob Seth 1685, acquired about 1820 by Edward Harris whose heirs Misses Mary and Sallie Harris renamed it "Bloomingdale". It passed under will of Miss Sallie Harris to her cousin Severn Teakle Wallis, one of Maryland's most distinguished sons. (1)

U.S. 50, east of Bloomingdale Road.

④ Bowlingly

Estate patented to James Bowling, 1658, and present manor house built 1733. East-west wing added about 1830. Before dawn, August 2, 1813, British Troops under Sir Charles James Napier landed here and after defeating the local militia seriously damaged the manor house and its contents before reembarking. (4)

Embert Avenue and Maryland Avenue, Queenstown.

⑤ Callister's Ferry

Near this spot Henry Callister, merchant, operated a rope and raft ferry across the Chester River during the 1750's and 1760's. Well into the next century the crossing at Crumpton continued to be known as "Callister's Ferry". It served as an important link in early overland transportation of the upper eastern shore. (57)

MD 290, south of bridge at Kent County Line.

⑥ Chesapeake College

This first regional college in Maryland and first two-year community college on the Eastern Shore was founded December 22, 1965, and classes began on the campus September, 1969. The sponsors include the State of Maryland and Caroline, Kent, Queen Anne's and Talbot Counties. (4)

U.S. 50, west of MD 213 and MD 662.

⑦ "Cheston on Wye"

Surveyed as "Cheston" 1659 for John and William Coursey containing 800 acres - six generations of Courseys (who adopted the older spelling of Decourcey) lived here and lie buried here. The original house was burned. (1)

Carmichael Road and Cheston Lane.

⑧ Christ Church
Town of Broad Creek

First Christian Congregation in Maryland organized 1632 by the Reverend Richard James at Kent Fort, south end of island. Church moved here ca. 1650. Rebuilt 1712 and 1826. This oldest continuous congregation in Maryland moved to Stevensville in 1880. (4)

MD 8, south of U.S. 50 and U.S. 301.

⑨ "Clover Field"
1622 Acres

Patented to William Hemsley in 1730 as a resurvey of several earlier tracts granted in the sixteen hundreds. The house contains some fine woodwork. The Hemsley graveyard has some interesting tombs. (1)

MD 662 and Foremans Landing Road.

⑩ The Courthouse
Queen Anne's County

Oldest courthouse in continuous use in the State of Maryland. The building was authorized by Acts of Assembly after the removal of the County Seat from Queenstown to Chester Mills, later Centreville. It was erected between 1791 and 1796 on land purchased from Elizabeth Nicholson on her portion of "Chesterfield", the estate of her grandfather, William Sweatman. (55)

MD 213, south of Broadway, Centreville.

⑪ Dudley's Chapel

Built in 1783 on land donated by Joshua Dudley. This is the first Methodist meeting house erected in Queen Anne's County, as an outgrowth of a Society organized in 1774. It is one of the earliest surviving Methodist Churches in Maryland. Bishops Francis Asbury, Thomas Coke and Richard Whatcoat preached here. The brick Chapel was renovated and restored to it's present appearance in 1883. It was listed on the National Register of Historic Places in 1979. (4)

2 miles west of Sudlersville on Benton Corner Road, 0.3 mile south of MD 300.

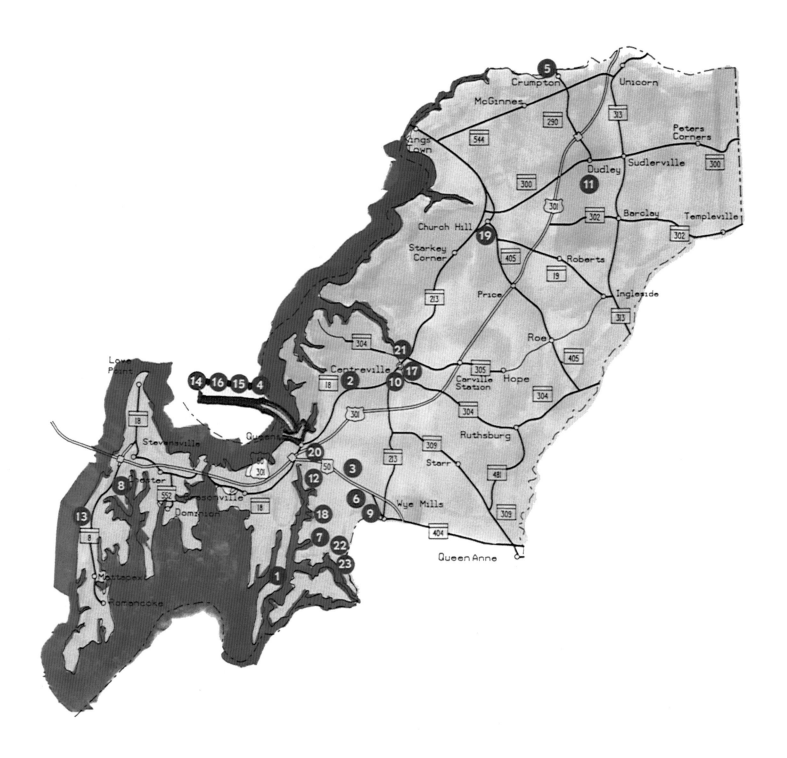

QUEEN ANNE'S COUNTY

Located south of Kent County and the Chester River is Queen Anne's County. Much like its surrounding counties, the economy is split between farms and the water. The rich farmland of the area attracted many early colonists.

12 ## Historic Points

Cheston-On-Wye, Stagwell, Wye Plantation, Wye Island. (1)

Carmichael Road, south of U.S. 50.

13 ## Kent Island

"The Isle of Kent"

William Claiborne of Virginia established a trading post, settlement and fort at the southern end of this island in 1631. Lord Baltimore's rights were resisted, which led to serious controversy until taken by armed forces in 1637. (1)

MD 8, south of U.S. 50 and U.S. 301.

14 ## "Lord's Gift"

1050 Acres

Granted to Henry Coursey 1658, 1000 acres by order of Lord Baltimore for "Conspicuous faithfulness to him during the late contest" (the Uprising of 1652 by Richard Bennett and William Claiborne). The 50 acres were for transporting himself into the Colony. This is the tract known as the "Thumbgrant" of legendary origin. (1)

MD 18, south of Queenstown.

15 ## "Morgan's Neck"

"Morgan's Neck" (300 acres) was patented by Cecil Calvert on January 26, 1658, to "Henry Morgan, of the Isle of Kent, Gentleman," for transporting into the province Frances Malyn and Francis Ash. The tract descended to his daughter Frances Sayer, in 1674; and to Elizabeth Rousby, his granddaughter, in 1698. Elizabeth Rousby married Richard Bennett, III, grandson of the puritan Governor of Virginia. Their dwelling nearby was excavated in 1973. (60)

Ice House Point Road, Queenstown.

16 ## Richard Bennett, III

1667-1749

His Wife Elizabeth Rousby

1682-1740

Bennett's Will (1749) Ordered 250 pounds sterling to be "Expended in a decent house to be built over the graveyard and burying

place where my dear wife lays interr'd." The Will (1698) of Frances Morgan Sayer ordered "a chapel built of lime and breek" (20 by 30 feet) over the grave of her husband, Col. Peter Sayer, at this site. Archaeological evidence indicates that the Sayer Chapel was most probably incorporated in the Bennett Chapel. Also buried here: Dorothy Blake Carroll (mother of Charles, the Barrister); Thomas Greene (D. 1674). (60)

Ice House Point Road, Queenstown.

17 ## Site of Goldsborough House

Circa 1798

By that year, a 2-story brick house, measuring 40 by 24 feet and described as "not yet fully complete," was built on a 4-acre lot of "Chesterfield", deeded in 1792 from Mary Nicholson to her daughter Henrietta. Henrietta's husband, Dr. John Bracco, died, and by 1799 she had married Dr. Robert Goldsborough. The property descended through the Goldsborough and McKenney families. The house was demolished in 1963. (60)

Happy Lady Lane and Railroad Avenue, Centreville.

18 ## Stagwell

Patented to Thomas Stagwell 1649. Acquired by Richard Bennett 1706, one of the largest land owners in Maryland. His descendant Judge Richard Bennett Carmichael built the house about 1805. He presided over the convention of 1867, for a new constitution for the State of Maryland. (1)

Carmichael Road, south of Stagwell Road.

19 ## St. Luke's Episcopal Parish

Founded 1728, when the Provincial Council in Annapolis granted a petition to establish the present parish. St. Luke's, the oldest brick church in the State with its original structure, was completed, 1732, at the cost of 140,000 pounds of tobacco. From 1692 until 1732 services were held in the up river chapel, located on the present site. All records are preserved intact, including births, baptisms, marriages, burials, vestry meetings and special occasions. (4)

Main Street, south of MD 19, Church Hill.

20 ## St. Peter's Church

(Roman Catholic)

Congregation first organized c. 1639 on nearby Kent Island by Rev. John Altham, S.J. St. Peter's was est. Feb. 3, 1765, by Rev. Joseph Mosely, S.J. of St. Joseph's, Talbot Co. A 1760 bequest of 50 lbs. from Edward Neale of "Bowlingly" provided $1^1/_2$ acre lot here, on which brick chapel was built before 1784. (Demolished 1960). Part of present structure begun 1823 by Rev. James Moynihan, completed 1827 by Rev. Peter Veulemans. The Aspe, Nave and Vestibule are major additions 1877 under Rev. Ed. Henchy. (56)

U.S. 50, east of Greenspring Road.

21 ## Wright's Chance

Early plantation house with original paneling. Listed as an "old dwelling" a 1744 resurvey of "Smith's Forrest", patented 1681. Moved, 1964, by the Queen Anne's County Historical Society to present site, part of "Chesterfield", upon which the town of Centreville was founded. (58)

MD 21, south of Water Street, Centreville.

22 ## Wye Island

Patented to Col. Philemon Lloyd as "Llyod's Insula" 1682, a combination of four earlier patents. Henrietta Maria Lloyd married Samuel Chew and their daughters married William Paca, 3rd Governor of Maryland, and John Beale Bordely, who inherited the island half to each from Philemon Lloyd Chew in 1770. (1)

Carmichael Road, south of Wye Plantation Marker.

23 ## "Wye Plantation"

Home of William Paca, signer of the Declaration of Independence and twice Governor of Maryland. Born at Chilbury Hall, Harford County 1740. Died and lies buried here, 1799. The unusual house probably dates about 1740. (1)

Carmichael Road, 1 mile south of Cheston Lane.

Caroline Courthouse

Denton Church

CAROLINE COURTHOUSE Caroline County was established in 1773 from parts of Queen Anne's and Dorchester Counties. This courthouse was founded in 1797 on a site then known as Pig Point and is now known as Denton. **DENTON CHURCH** - is just one of the many remarkable buildings in Denton. Caroline County was named in honor of Caroline Calvert a sister of Frederick, the last Lord Baltimore. (See page 71, markers 1 and 5).

CAROLINE COUNTY

1   Caroline Courthouse

Caroline County-established, 1773, from parts of Queen Anne's and Dorchester Counties - held its early courts at seven different locations until 1797 when its first courthouse was built on this site, once known as Pig Point. The 1895 replacement was renovated and extensively added to, 1966. The courthouse was purchased, 1791, for 120 shillings.   (4)

Market Street between 1st and 2nd Streets, Denton.

2   Charles Dickenson

Born here on Wiltshire Manor in Caroline County in 1780. Moved to Foxley Hall, Easton in 1795. He read law under Judge Marshall. He met Andrew Jackson traveling across the Eastern Shore to the United States Congress. He moved to Nashville, Tennessee. Killed by Jackson in a duel May 30, 1806 in the Red River Valley of Kentucky. Body returned here by Truxton, faithful negro servant. Lead casket found 500 yards east of this spot December 1, 1965.   (10)

MD 16 and MD 621.

3   Choptank

Before 1679, Indians had a settlement here. Present village stands on parts of tracks once known as Paradise, Belmont, Huntington and Gore. Community was "Leonard's Warf" c.1855 and "Medford's Wharf" later. In 1883 Choptank Post Office was established, named for both the Indian Tribe and the River. Shipping and industry spurred growth during the 1880's.   (13)

CO. 194 at Choptank Creek and Poplar Neck Roads.

4   Colonel William Richardson
Born 1735 - Died 1825

Member Maryland Assembly 1773-76. Introduced bill forming Caroline County 1774 of which he was one of the Commissioners. Colonel of the "Flying Camp" of the Eastern Shore 1776. Fought at Harlem Heights. First Colonel 5th Maryland

Regiment. Moved Continental Treasury from Philadelphia to Baltimore 1777. Helped suppress Tory Rebellions in lower Eastern Shore. Presidential Elector 1789-93. Lived and lies buried at Gilpin's Point.   (1)

MD 16, 2 miles north of Harmony.

5   Denton

Originally called "Edenton" for Robert Eden, Maryland's last Colonial Governor. Caroline County was named in honor of his wife Caroline Calvert, a sister of Frederick, the last Lord Baltimore.   (1)

MD 404 and MD 313, Denton.

6   Goldsborough House

Judge Laird Goldsborough lived here 1897-1970. As onetime Adjutant General of the Philippines he authored the Island's first Constitution. Part of the house is of pre-revolutionary construction. Among other members of this Caroline County family distinguished for public service: W. E. Goldsborough, U.S. Consult, Amoy, China; T. Alan Goldsborough, longtime U.S. Congress-man and Federal Judge; Dr. G. Winder Goldsborough, General Practitioner and State Legislator; and Elwell Goldsborough nationally famous Electrical Engineer.   (4)

MD 314, east of Church Street, Greensboro.

7   Greensboro

Founded 1732 as Bridge Town, then in Queen Anne's and Dorchester Counties. Named Greensboro 1791. Sessions of Caroline County Court held here November, December, 1778; June, 1779; March, 1780. Choptank Bridge, the first across the river, built near here before 1732.   (4)

MD 313 and MD 314, south of bridge, Greensboro.

8   Linchester - Circa 1681

Since the establishment of Hunting Creek Grist Mill prior to 1681, a mill on this site has served farmers. Known during the

Revolutionary War as Murray's Mill, it supplied provisions to the Continental Army. Linchester also was a Colonial Port of Entry.   (4)

MD 318, 1 mile southeast of Preston.

9   Peter Harrington
Revolutionary Officer, founder of Greensboro

Son of Nathan Harrington and grandson of Peter Rich, early landowners here. He served in 1778 as 2nd Lieutenant, 28th Battalion of Militia, Caroline County. In 1783, he successfully laid out town on tract called Ingram's Desire (efforts to sell lots beside Choptank Bridge in 1732 having failed). He built brick house, Church and Bernard Avenues, 1786-1789. After his death in 1814, he was buried in this yard which he had donated for Methodist Meeting House in 1789. Nearby are graves of his younger son Alexander and daughter Mary.   (5)

MD 480 at Main Street and Cedar Lane, Greensboro.

10   Preston

Started 1846 around Frazier's Chapel, an early Methodist Church, the land for which was purchased 1797. First called "Snowhill", the name was changed to Preston 1856, in honor of a prominent Baltimore lawyer. Preston was chartered as a town in 1892. (1)

Maple Street, Preston.

11   Neck Meeting House

Neck or Tuckahoe Neck Meeting House was built in 1802 by members of the Society of Friends who had been Nicholites, a sect that originated in Caroline County. The building was used as a house of worship and as a Friends School until 1897. The building was then rented by "Dunkards" for religious meetings for black persons and as a school. It was privately sold in 1901 and since 1949 has been owned by Choptank Electric Cooperative, Inc.   (11)

MD 328 and MD 404.

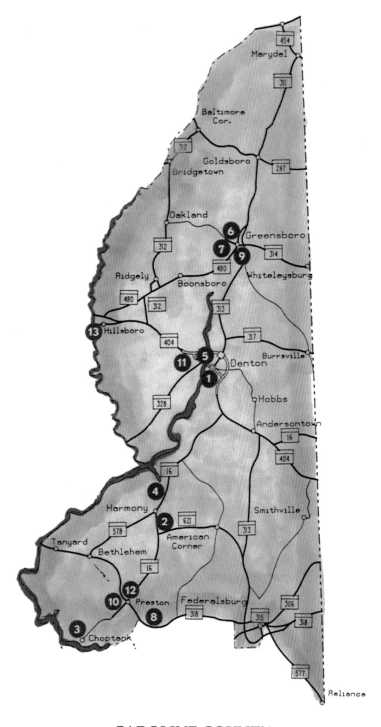

CAROLINE COUNTY

Caroline County is a rather long county running along the east boundaries of both Queen Anne's County and Talbot County. It is the only Eastern Shore county which does not have frontage on the bay or the ocean. Large meandering rivers flow through the county affording the residents great bass fishing and water for productive farms.

12 Site of Frazier's Chapel
Preston, Maryland 1785

Built by Rev. Freeborn Garrettson and Captain William Frazier. Early Methodist Pastors included Jesse Lee, Joseph Everette and Bishops Francis Asbury and John Emory. Remodeled and named Bethesda 1849. Present church built 1875. Rebuilt 1958. (4)
MD 16 and MD 331, Preston.

13 St. Paul's Episcopal Church
(St. John's Parish)

Established 1748 at nearby Tuckahoe Bridge in Queen Anne's County. Congregation built church here in 1768, but it fell into decline as influence of Methodism grew on Eastern Shore. Under guidance of Rev. Robert William Goldsborough, present gothic revival structure was begun 1853, patterned after design of Richard Upjohn. Despite destructive windstorm, church was completed, consecrated in 1858. (12)
Church Street, Hillsboro.

NECK MEETING HOUSE - or Tuckahoe Neck Meeting House was built in 1802 by members of the
Society of Friends. The house was used as a house of worship and as the Friends School.
(See page 71, marker 11).

The Talbot Resolves

The Wye Oak

THE TALBOT RESOLVE - was declared two years before the Declaration of Independence. The citizens of Talbot County met on this site to protest Great Britain's closing of the Port of Boston. This location is now the county seat and the courthouse of Talbot County. (See page 77, marker 22).

THE WYE OAK - The largest White Oak in the United States. Estimated at being 400 years old in 1940. (See page 77, marker 28).

TALBOT COUNTY

1 Betty's Cove Meeting House

Near this spot, about 1665, Quaker Settlers built the Betty's Cove Meeting House. At this intersection, known as "The Pincushion", they established a school. Adding one of the first public libraries in America in 1676. George Fox, founder of the Society of Friends, visited Betty's Cove twice in 1672, when there were "so many boats upon the river it was almost like the Thames," as Quakers came to meeting. (4)

MD 370 and MD 33.

2 "Cantebury Manor"
1000 Acres

Laid out for Richard Tilgman Chirurgeon as "Manor of Tilghman's Fortune" 20th July 1658. Sold by him to Richard Preston 30 September, 1665, as the "Manor of Cantebury" "together with all royaltys and privileges most usually belonging to Manors in England". (1)

Bailey's Neck Road, 1 mile west of MD 333.

3 "Compton"

Patented 1664 to James Elvard. Acquired by William Stevens before 1700. His grandson Samuel Stevens, Jr. member of Legislature 1808 to 1820. Governor of Maryland 1822 to 1825. During his administration Jews were enfranchised. When Lafayette visited America 1824-1825 Governor Stevens met him at Fort McHenry, Baltimore. (1)

U.S. 50 and MD 565.

4 "Crosiadore"

Originally patented 1659 as "Crois Dower", 1667 "Crois Dower Marsh" and 1695 "Crosedore Addition". John Dickinson was born here, 1732. He was the author of (1768) "Letters from a farmer in Pennsylvania to the inhabitants of the British Colonies". Crosiadore is still (1938) in the Dickinson Family. In 1738 Dickinson College, Carlisle, Pennsylvania, was named for John Dickinson. (1)

U.S. 50 and MD 565.

5 Fausley

Birthplace of Lieutenant Colonel Tench Tilgman, Christmas day 1744. Aide-de-Camp to General George Washington, 1776-1783, and a participant in every major campaign of the main army in the American Revolution. He was entrusted to carry the official terms of the surrender at Yorktown to the Continental Congress in Philadelphia. Died, Baltimore, April 18, 1786. Buried, Oxford Cemetery. (43)

Villa Road, west of Goldsborough Neck Road.

6 Frederick Douglass
1817- 1895 Negro Patriot

Attained freedom and devoted his life and talents to the abolition of slavery and the cause of universal suffrage. Visited England in 1845 and in 1859. Won many prominent friends abroad and at home. Was U.S. Marshall for the District of Columbia and U.S. Minister to Haiti. Was born in Tuckahoe, Talbot County. (1)

MD 328, west of bridge over Tuckahoe River.

7 Grave of General Perry Benson
1757- 1827

A leader in his home community and state. In the Revolutionary War he served as a Captain, and was wounded twice. In the War of 1812, he commanded the militia in Talbot, Caroline, and Dorchester Counties. (4)

Station Road, south of MD 33.

8 "Hole-In-The-Wall"

Early name of this village derived from a famous Inn here of that title. Called after a well-known English Tavern of about 1720. Robert Morris, father of the financier of the Revolution lies buried near the ruins of White Marsh Church. (1)

U.S. 50 and Hole-In-The-Wall Road.

9 Little Red Schoolhouse

The only one-room schoolhouse remaining in Talbot County is a half-mile southwest of Longwoods. Erected ca. 1885. The Talbot County Commissioners restored it in 1969 as a museum showing the development of education in the area. (4)

U.S. 50 and MD 662.

10 "The Manour of Ratcliffe"

800 Acres patented January 17, 1659 to Robert Morris of London, mariner, "together with a Court Baron and all things there unto belonging by the laws and customs of England". One of the earliest grants on the Eastern Shore. (1)

MD 17, 3 miles west of Easton.

11 Matthew Tilghman
1718 - 1790

Here lived the planter and patriot called "Father of the Revolution in Maryland". Speaker, Maryland Assembly, 1773-1774. President, Maryland Conventions and Chairman of Council of Safety, 1774-1776. Having headed each Maryland Delegation to Continental Congress, 1774-1776, he returned to Annapolis to preside over state convention that wrote Maryland's first Constitution. (42)

Rich Neck Road, north of MD 451.

12 Nathaniel Hopkins

Leader of his people who was born a slave circa 1830; fought for Union in Civil War; originated annual Trappe Emancipation Day Celebration, 1867, and headed it until his death in 1900. One of the founders of Scott's Methodist Church. Helped establish first "colored schools" at Trappe and Barber. Buried in Old Paradise Cemetery on this site. (41)

U.S. 50 and Barber Road.

13 Old White Marsh Episcopal Church

Original structure built before 1690. Early 18th century rector was the Reverend Daniel Maynadier. A later provincial rector (1746 - 1768), the Reverend Thomas Bacon, compiled "Bacon's Laws", authoritative compendium of Colonial Statutes. Thomas John Claggett, first Episcopal Bishop of Maryland officiated here in 1793; Robert Morris, Sr., father of Revolutionary Financier, is buried here. Church burned in 1892, was partially restored in 1977. (4)

U.S. 50 and Hole-In-The-Wall Road.

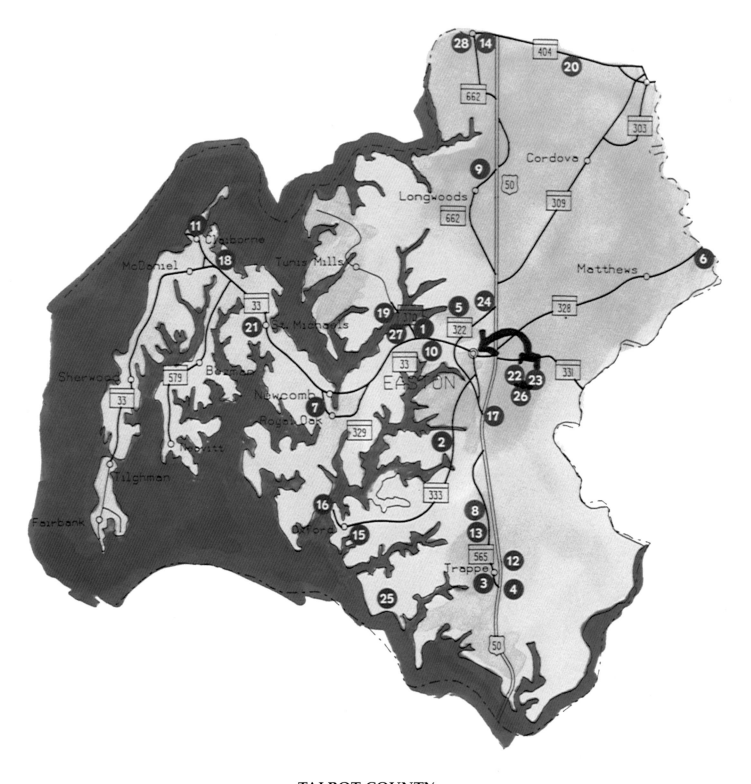

TALBOT COUNTY

Talbot County is located south of Queen Anne's County and west of Caroline County. It is the high point of Eastern Shore culture and lifestyle. Everything in the county is close to a river, bay, creek, or inlet of some sort. The Tred Avon Ferry, which links Oxford and St. Michaels, has run longer than any other ferry in the country.

🄮 Old Wye Episcopal Church

Only remaining Anglican Church in Talbot County. Built 1721 as a Chapel-of-Ease by donations of 60,000 pounds of tobacco and 100 pounds sterling. Originally named St. Luke's, it was a place of worship until 1829. Reconstructed in 1854, but later fell into disrepair until restored in 1949 to original design with high box pews, hanging side pulpit and gallery with original Royal Arms.   (44)

MD 662 and MD 404.

🄯 Oxford

One of the first towns and ports authorized by Assembly in 1683. Called "William-Stadt" in 1695. Robert Morris, father of the financier of the Revolution, lived here until his death in 1750. He is buried at Old Whitmarsh Church.   (1)

MD 333, Oxford.

🄰 Oxford-Bellevue Ferry
October 1760

Believed to be nation's oldest ferry service in continuous operation. Ferry has plied across Tred Avon River between Oxford and Bellevue since service was started by Mrs. Elizabeth Skinner in October 1760 with scow propelled rowing and sculling.   (4)

MD 333 (Morris Street) and Strand Street, Oxford.

🄱 Peachblossom Meetinghouse

Built 1880 by people of Swedenburg, Lutheran, Methodist, and Brethren Faiths near Peachblossom Creek and used by each denomination every forth Sunday. The building, originally known as Peachblossom Meeting House, was so named because the first Peach Trees in Maryland were planted near this site. Now known as Little Round Top Church. It is owned solely by the Church of the Brethren.   (4)

U.S. 50, south of MD 322.

🄲 Second Defense of St. Michaels

Here, August 26, 1813, General Perry Benson, with 600 militia, most of them from Talbot County, halted a British force of 1,800. The Easton Artillery manned the road, the 4th and 26th Infantry the woods, and the 9th Cavalry the wings.   (4)

MD 33, 0.8 mile east of MD 579.

🄳 Site of "The Rest"

"The Rest" was the home of Admiral Franklin Buchanan, 1800-1874, First Superintendent of the Naval Academy, 1845, Commander of the Washington Navy Yard, 1861. Commander of the Confederate Iron-Clads Virginia, 1862, and Tennessee, 1864, and Senior Officer in the Confederate Navy.   (7)

MD 370 at Rest Road.

🄴 St. Joseph's Church

Originally a mission of Old Bohemia founded March 18, 1765, by Father Joseph Mosley, S.J. Oldest section built 1782, additions made 1848 and 1903. Father Mosley one of three priests interred under Chapel. Since 1868, except during wars, annual jousting tournaments held here on first Wednesday of August.   (4)

MD 404 and Church Lane.

🄵 St. Michaels

This town was attacked by a British force during the night of August 10, 1813, but they were driven back to their boats at sunrise. A gun used in its defense is mounted in the town square.   (1)

MD 33, east of Seymour Avenue (on school grounds).

🄶 The Talbot Resolves
(May 24, 1774)

Two years before the Declaration of Independence, the citizens of Talbot County met on this site to protest Great Britian's closing of the Port of Boston, and resolved "to act as friends to liberty and the general interests of mankind".   (4)

MD 565 on the Courthouse Lawn.

🄷 Third Haven
(Meeting House of the Society of Friends 1682-1684)

One of the oldest frame houses of worship in the United States. In continuous use since it was built.   (4)

MD 565, north of MD 333.

🄸 Tilgman's Fortune

This farmhouse, built about 1800 by Captain Clement Vickers, a bay boat owner and operator, was moved to this site from Tilgman's Fortune, an original Manor Grant dated 1659 and located about 5 miles to the southwest. It was restored by the Talbot County Chamber of Commerce, January 1969.   (4)

U.S. 50, 0.5 mile north of Black Dog Alley Road.

🄹 "The Wilderness"

Part of present house, a lower wing, built c. 1700. Home of Daniel Martin and his son Nicholas, who was captain in 38th Battalion of Maryland Militia during Revolutionary War and died here in 1808. Nicholas Martin's son Daniel, elected Governor of Maryland in 1829 and again in 1831. Added larger portion of the house c. 1810.   (5)

Island Creek Road, west of Trappe.

🄺 William Penn

In December 1682 attended a general meeting of "Friends" on the Choptank River after a visit to Lord Baltimore at Colonel Thomas Tailler's in Ann Arundel County. "Philemon Lloyd with some horsemen waited on Penn" by order of Lord Baltimore.   (1)

Old Third Haven Meeting House at Easton.

🄻 Wye House

Ancestral seat of the Lloyds of Maryland since 1661. Nine generations of this family active and influential in Province and State have lived here and ten generations lie buried here.   (1)

MD 370 at MD 33.

🄼 The Wye Oak

The largest White Oak in the United States. Estimated to be 400 years old (1940). Deeded to the Sate of Maryland September 20, 1939, and made a State Park.   (1)

MD 662, south of MD 404.

Glasgow

Dorchester County Courthouse

East New Market

GLASGOW - was built in 1760 and is the birthplace of William Vans Murray, who was appointed minister to the Hague by President Washington in 1782. **DORCHESTER COUNTY COURTHOUSE** - The original courthouse built in 1687 was destroyed by fire. The present courthouse was built in 1854. **EAST NEW MARKET** - is now the site of numerous historic houses, however this area was originally an Indian trading post. (See page 79, markers 3, 6, 7, and 10).

DORCHESTER COUNTY

❶ "Appleby"

The home of Governor Thomas Holliday Hicks. Born 1798. Died 1865. Governor of Maryland 1858-62. U.S. Senator 1862-65. (1)

MD 341, north of Burton Street, Cambridge.

❷ Bethlehem Methodist Episcopal Church
(Built 1787 - Rebuilt 1857)

The original chapel was built on this site which was donated by Moses and Elizabeth Le Compte. The deed, dated September 15, 1787, is the oldest one on record for Methodist Episcopal Church Land in Dorchester County. Both Bishop Francis Asbury and Reverend Freeborn Garrettson preached here. (4)

Hooper Neck Road, north of Bay Shore Road, Taylor Island.

❸ Cambridge

Originally part of the Choptank Indian Reservation laid out for them in 1669. Cambridge was made a Port of Entry by the Assembly in 1684. It is one of the few towns authorized at that early date that has survived. (1)

U.S. 50, south of bridge, Cambridge.

❹ Chapel of Ease, Old Trinity Episcopal Church
circa 1707

In the selection of the middle point between the Atlantic Ocean and the Chesapeake Bay for the start of the Mason-Dixon line survey. This area was the center of a long controversy among British, Maryland and Pennsylvania Officials as to whether Taylor's Island was a part of the mainland or an island. An adverse decision resulted in the loss of land to Pennsylvania, now Delaware. (4)

Hooper Neck Road, 0.5 mile south of Bay Shore Road, Taylors Island.

❺ Choptank Indian Reservation

Set aside by State in 1669 extending from Cambridge to Secretary Creek along Choptank River and three miles back into the woods for the Indians whose kings were "Ababco", "Hataswapp" and "Tequassimo". (1)

1 mile east of East New Market, on road leading to Secretary.

❻ Dorchester County Courthouse

The first Courthouse, a two-story wooden building, stood from 1687 to about 1771 and measured 40 by 24 feet. It was razed and a larger Courthouse, authorized by the General Assembly in 1771, was built on an adjoining lot. It stood until May 9, 1852 when it was destroyed by fire. The present courthouse, completed in 1854, was in the Italian villa style by Richard Upjohn of Boston. William A. Stone, Jr., designed the rear addition in 1931. (79)

206 High Street, Cambridge.

❼ East New Market
Settled 1660 on North-South Choptank Indian Trail

Originally "Crossroads," later "New Market." Post for trading with Indians erected 1767. In Revolutionary, "New Market Blues," volunteer Militiamen, were organized in this supply center for Continental Army. South on Main Street is "Old House of the Hinges," so-called because of outbuilding's ironwork. Home of Major Anthony Manning, who served in War of 1812, and his son, Dr. Anthony Manning, Union Surgeon in Civil War. By the 1780's, a center of American Methodism. Former New Market Academy founded 1818. Renamed "East New Market" in 1827. Incorporated 1884. (77)

MD 14 and MD 16.

❽ Friendship Hall
(circa 1740)

Fine 2 1/2 story brick house with pilasters on front and two oval windows in pediment of west gable. Home of Sulivane Family, 17th century settlers here. There generations of whom served in Maryland General Assembly: James Sulivane, Commissary Officer in Revolutionary War who, with Thomas Logan, organized "New Market Blues," Dr. Daniel Sulivane, elected to House of Delegates 1824, and Colonel Clement Sulivane, lawyer and, Confederate Veteran. (76)

MD 14, east of MD 16.

❾ Gary's Creek - Indian Path
Dorchester County

Gary's Creek was named for Stephen Gary (D. 1686), High Sheriff and one of the Judges of Dorchester County for whom "Spocott" was surveyed on this creek December 27, 1662. This road about 1663 was the Indian path from the Indian towns on Choptank River to Jordans Point (Mill's Point) on Chesapeake Bay. (4)

MD 343, west of Richardson Road, near Llyods.

❿ Glasgow
(Built 1760)

Birthplace of William Vans Murray. Appointed minister to the Hague by President George Washington, March 2, 1787. He served until 1801. He was Minister Plenipotentiary to Paris as one of the negotiators of the Treaty with France, signed in 1800, which averted war. (4)

Hambrooks Blvd., west of Queen Anne Avenue, Cambridge.

⓫ Harriet Tubman
1820 - 1913

The "Moses of her people." Harriet Tubman of the Bucktown District found freedom for herself and some three hundred other slaves whom she led north. In the Civil War she served the Union Army as a nurse, scout and spy. (7)

Greenbrier Road, 1 mile west of Bestpitch Ferry Road, near Bucktown.

DORCHESTER COUNTY

Sitting south of the historic Choptank River and Talbot County is Dorchester County. The center of most of the history and culture in the county is located in Cambridge. The rural landscape is composed of miles and miles of marshlands and flat farmland.

12 ## Hoopers Island

Long a community of watermen. This chain of islands bears name of family who settled in Dorchester County from southern Maryland in latter part of 17th century. Active in Colonial affairs in 18th Century was Col. Henry Hooper, whose seat was "Warwick Fort Manor" near Secretary. His son, Brig. Gen. Henry Hooper, as Commander of Militia for Lower Eastern Shore was responsible for defense of this region during the Revolution.   (5)

MD 335, south of Bridge.

13 ## My Lady Sewall's Manor

Central part of house built shortly after grant of 2,000 acres in 1661 to Henry Sewall of London, Secretary of the Province. He died in 1665. His widow, Jane, came to Maryland on same ship as Governor Charles Calvert (afterwards 3rd Lord Baltimore), whom she married in 1666. Early 18th Century paneling from house is in Brooklyn, N.Y., Museum of Art. In 1720, Col. Henry Hooper bought 1,243 acres of this manor from Maj. Nicholas Sewall, adding land to Warwick Fort Manor.   (130)

North of MD 14, parking lot at end of Willows Street, Secretary.

14 ## Patty Cannon's House

At Johnson's Cross Roads where the noted kidnapping group had headquarters as described in George Alfred Townsend's novel "The Entailed Hat". The house borders on Caroline and Dorchester Counties and the State of Delaware.   (1)

MD 392, west of MD 577, Reliance

15 ## "Rehoboth"

Patented by Captain John Lee of Virginia, 1673, for 2350 acres. It descended through the Lee Family until 1787. Thomas Sim Lee, 1745-1819, (second Governor of Maryland) was descended from the Lees of Rehoboth.   (1)

MD 1 and MD 313, Eldorado.

16 ## Spocott Windmill

This windmill is typical of the grist post mills used in the 18th and 19th Centuries for grinding grain. Such a windmill, built here about 1850 by John A. L. Radcliffe, was blown down in the blizzard of 1888. In 1972 it was reconstructed, using the original grinding stones and internal steps.   (4)

MD 343, west of Richardson Road, Lloyds .

17 ## "Stanley Institute"

Oldest community-owned one-room school-house still intact in Dorchester County. First constructed c. 1865 near Church Creek. Moved here in 1867. It was used continuously until July 15, 1966, as Rock Elementary School for students in grades 1 through 7. Many ministers of Delaware Annual Conference of Methodist Church received their primary education here. School named for Ezekriel Stanley, President of its First Board. Other trustees included Dennis Camper, Jr., Charles F. Kiah, Moses Opher and Nathaniel Young.   (78)

MD 16 at Bayley Road, Church Creek.

18 ## Thomas Holiday Hicks
1798 - 1865

In this cemetery is the grave of Thomas Holliday Hicks, Governor of Maryland 1858-1862, and United State Senator from Maryland 1862-1865. At the beginning of the Civil War during his tenure as Governor, the position of Maryland was more important nationally than at any time in its histroy. But for him Maryland might have joined the secession movement.   (7)

Cambridge Cemetery in Hicks Family Graveyard.

19 ## Trinity Episcopal Church
Dorchester Parish
Church Creek, Maryland

Built about 1675, Old Trinity is the Nation's oldest church standing in its original form and still regularly used by its congregation. Typical of the faithful restoration done in 1953-60 are the "three-decker" pulpit pew, the highbacked box pews made of Southern Pine salvaged from abandoned Maryland and Virginia 18th century houses and the altar rail of native Black Walnut. The large red brick floor tiles and the altar table frame are original. A unique feature of this small brick church is the semicircular sanctuary with a six-foot radius. Buried in the cemetery are many soldiers of the Revolution. Open Wed. - Mon. from Mar. - Dec. and Sat. - Sun. from Jan. Feb.   (80)

Taylors Island Road, near Church Creek and MD 16.

20 ## "Tubman Chapel"
St. Mary Star of the Sea Parish

Probably oldest surviving Roman Catholic Church on lower eastern shore. Begun by Richard Tubman, II on land he provided c. 1769, when Rev. Joseph Mosley, S. J. of St. Joseph's, Talbot County, reorganized congregation here. (Catholics had worshiped in area since mid-17th century, served from across Chesapeake Bay.) Chapel enlarged c. 1817 by Rev. James Moynihan, further renovated 1867 by Rev. Ed. Henchy, S.J.   (4)

MD 335, east of Meekins Neck Road.

21 ## Unnacokossimmon
Explorer to the Nanticoke Indians

Lived (about 1677) at Chicacone, an ancient Indian town north of this point. The Nanticoke Indian Reservation was laid out by Act of Assembly 1698, containing 5166 $1/4$ acres.   (1)

MD 331, north of U.S. 50, near Vienna.

Teakle Mansion

Crisfield

Teakle Mansion

CRISFIELD - located near the bottom of Somerset County, Crisfield is renowned as being the seafood capital of Maryland. Boats leave Crisfield daily for Smith Island (see page 83, markers 15 and 16)
TEAKLE MANSION - is located in the town of Princess Anne, and is one of the finest mansions on the Eastern Shore. (See page 83, markers 10).

SOMERSET COUNTY

❶ Birthplace of Samuel Chase
17 April 1741 - 19 June 1811

Signer of the Declaration of Independence. Judge of the General Court of Maryland 1781. Judge of Baltimore County Court 1793. Judge of the U.S. Supreme Court 1796. (1)
U.S. 13 and MD 362.

❷ Colonel George Gale
1671 - 1712

About 2 miles southwest is "Tusculum" on Monie Creek. Plantation where Gale lived and lies buried (not open to the public). Born in Whitehaven, England, he settled in Maryland in 1701. His 3 vessels traded regularly between his native and adopted lands. His first wife was Mildred Warner Washington, widow of Lawrence Washington, and General George Washington's grandmother. She died on trip with Colonel Gale to Whitehaven, England, and is buried in St. Nicholas' Churchyard there. Gale was a devoted parent to his Washington stepchildren. (5)
MD 362, west of Black Road.

❸ Court House Hill

Site of second known Court House of Somerset County. On March 1, 1694, the Court purchased land near Dividing Creek and erected a structure 50 feet by 20 feet, "with gable ends of brick". The Court House functioned until 1742. (4)
MD 364 and Court House Hill Road.

❹ First Site of Washington Academy

A forerunner of Washington High School, the Academy was founded and built, 1767, under the Propriety Laws of 1694, enlarged, 1776, and destroyed by fire, 1797. Originally called Somerset Academy, it as renamed and chartered as Washington Academy, 1779. (4)
U.S. 13, south of Princess Anne, on Sign Post Road.

❺ General Arnold Elzey, C.S.A.
1816 - 1871

Born at "Elmwood", and a graduate of West Point, Arnold Elzey (Jones) entered the Civil War, April, 1861, with the First Maryland Infantry, C.S.A. At First Manassas he was commissioned Brigadier General. He served under General Stonewall Jackson and John Bell Hood. (7)
MD 627, Oriole.

❻ Joshua Thomas
1776 - 1853

Born Potato Neck, Somerset County. Named "Parson of the Islands" by British Troops at Tangier Island. As their Pastor predicted their defeat at Baltimore, 1814. Spread Methodism on Tangier, Deal, Saxis and Spring Islands. Buried beside this Chapel which bears his name. (4)
MD 363, Deal's Island.

❼ Kingston Hall

Built in 1731 by Robert King. Birthplace of Thomas King Carrol, Governor of Maryland, 1830-1831. Anna Ella Carroll, 1815 - 1894, known as the unofficial member of Lincoln's Cabinet, was born here. (4)
MD 413, north of Kingston.

❽ Make Peace

Patented for 150 acres 1678 to John Roach. The brick house on this property is one of the finest examples of very early colonial architecture on the Eastern Shore. (1)
MD 380, south of Johnson Creek Road.

❾ Manokin Presbyterian Church

One of five churches organized by the Reverend Francis Makemie in 1683. First preaching on this ground, 1672. Original church constructed prior to 1692. Present walls erected 1765. Tower added 1888. (4)
MD 675 and Fluers Lane, Princess Anne.

❿ Princess Anne Town
Founded 1732

Seat of Somerset County, erected 1666, and home of Samuel Chase, Signer of the Declaration of Independence. Near by are Washington Tavern, 1744; Manokin Presbyterian Church, 1762; St. Andrew's Episcopal Church, 1770; "Beckford", 1776; and Teackle Mansion, 1801. (4)
U.S. 13 and MD 363.

⓫ "Rehoboth"
("There is room")

1000 Acres surveyed 1665 for Colonel William Stevens, member of Governor's Council, through whose influence Francis Makemie came to Maryland and established Presbyterianism in the State. On this same tract stood the Episcopal Church of Coventry Parish. (1)
U.S. 13 and MD 667.

⓬ Rehoboth Presbyterian Church

Here in 1683 Reverend Francis Makemie began his ministry and in 1706 built this church, ruins of Coventry Episcopal Church. (1)
MD 667 at Rehoboth Road.

⓭ Saint Andrew's Episcopal Church
Somerset Parish

Parish established in 1692. St. Andrew's a Chapel-of-Ease to All Saint's Church, Monie, was built in 1770 and consecrated in 1845. Tower erected 1859; spire and chapel 1893; wall and lich gate 1964. (4)
South Beckford Avenue, north of Washington Street.

⓮ Saint Stephen's Church
Coventry Parish

Established by the Maryland General Assembly, June, 1751, near Cottingham's Ferry, Worcester County. On the same site, a new church, consecrated by the Right Reverend William R. Whittingham, Bishop of Maryland, December, 1849, was subsequently moved to Upper Fairmount and used until 1934. (4)
MD 361, near Upper Fairmount.

⓯ Smith Island

Chartered by Captain John Smith in 1608. Settled in 1657 by dissenters from St. Clements Island. Here Joshula Thomas, Parson of the Islands, converted many to the Methodist Faith. Smith Island consists of 3 distinct communities: Tylerton, Rhodes (formerly Rogues) Point, and Ewell. (4)
Jones Road and Somerset Road, Smith Island.

⓰ Ye Old St. Peters Methodist Church
Founded 1782

Joshua Thomas "Parson of the Islands" preached his first sermon in this church. His spiritual birthplace, the site of his conversion in 1807, is 300 yards south. "The Methodist", his famous log canoe, was launched about 500 yards to the north. (4)
MD 667, Jacksonville Road, near Crisfield.

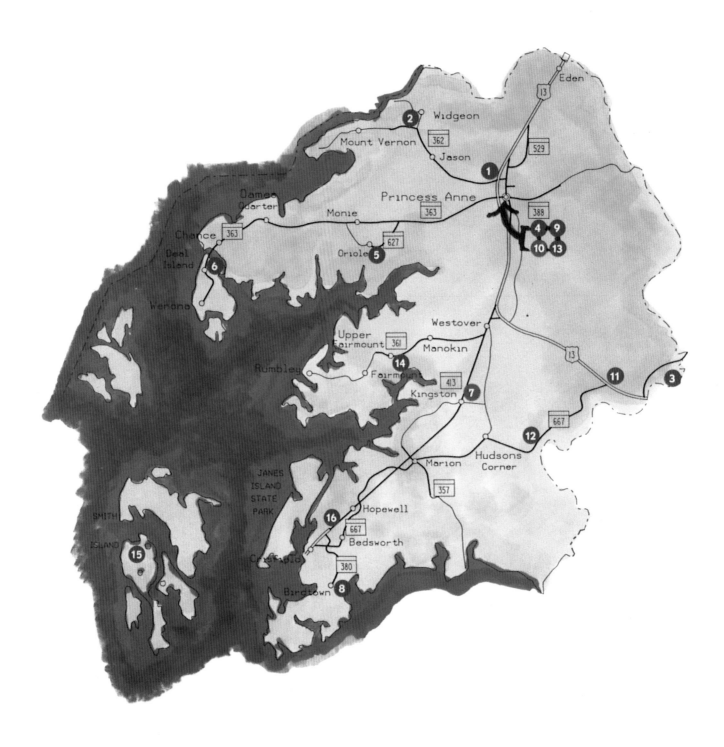

SOMERSET COUNTY

Somerset County is south of everything on the Eastern shore. Much like its neighboring counties, life in Somerset County centers on the water and the farm. The town of Chrisfield, in the south, could be called the "seafood capital" of the state.

DEAL'S ISLAND - is one of the most picturesque places in the state. Joshua Thomas, the pastor of the island, (from 1776 to 1853) predicted the defeat of the British at Baltimore in 1814.
(See page 83, marker 6).

Poplar Hill Mansion

Newtown Historic District

POPLAR HILL MANSION - was built circa 1805, bought by the State of Maryland in 1974, and restored by Wicomico County. **NEWTOWN HISTORIC DISTRICT** - contains some of the finest examples of Victorian and Federal houses on the Eastern Shore. (See page 87 markers 4 and 8).

WICOMICO COUNTY

❶ Birthplace of Samuel Chase
April 17, 1741 -June 19, 1811

Signer of the Declaration of Independence; Judge of the General Court of Maryland - 1781; Judge of Baltimore County Court - 1793; Judge of the U.S. Supreme Court - 1796. (1)
MD 529, 3.6 miles west of Allen.

❷ General John Henry Winder
C.S.A.

Born near Nanticoke, John Henry Winder was successively a graduate and instructor in West Point. A veteran of the Seminole and Mexican Wars, General Winder joined the Confederacy in 1861 and eventually directed all confederate military prisons east of the Mississippi. (7)
U.S. 13, Salisbury, south of Locust Street.

❸ Green Hill Town and Port

Authorized by Act of Assembly 1706 (one of 6 ports) "where vessels shall unlade Negroes wares, merchandizes and commodities". 100 acres to be laid out in lots with open spaces left for church, market place, and public buildings. Present church built in 1733. (1)
MD 349 and U.S. 50, Salisbury.

❹ Newton Historic District

Established by ordinance in 1975, Newton is distinguished by residential reconstruction after the two severe fires in 1860 and 1886. The district contains fine Victorian architecture and a notable example of the Federal Period. Poplar Hill Mansion, circa 1800, oldest surviving building in Salisbury. (15)
Oakdale and Division Streets, Salisbury. Division Street, between Broad and Chestnut Streets.

❺ Old Green Hill Church

Now St. Bartholomew's Episcopal Church, Parish Church of Stepney Parish, which was laid out in 1692. This building was erected in 1733 replacing the first building, a log church erected about 1694, which stood about 150 yards north of the present site. (4)
U.S. 50 and MD 347, Hebron.

❻ "Old Spring Hill"
St. Paul's Church

Established here between 1711 and 1725 as a Chapel of Ease for Green Hill Church (1694) located 8 miles south of the Wicomico River. The present edifice was completed in 1773 to replace the original structure. Some of the original furnishings are still in use. (4)
U.S. 50 and MD 347.

❼ Pemberton Hall

Built in 1741 by Colonel Isaac Handy, planter, lawyer, founder of Salisbury and officer of the local militia during the Revolution. He had operated a lumber business at Handy's Landing at the head of the Wicomico River where, in 1732, Salisbury Town was established. (5)
Pemberton Road, (CO. 70) and east of Crooked Lane.

❽ Poplar Hill Mansion

"Poplar Hill Mansion" (traditional name thought to be of the 19th Century origin) was built circa 1805. It was accepted for the National Register of Historic Places on October 7, 1971. The property was purchased by the State of Maryland in 1974 and subsequently restored by Wicomico County. The City of Salisbury now owns and maintains Poplar Hill Mansion. (158)
117 Elizabeth St., off U.S. 13 North, Salisbury.

❾ Rockwalkin School circa 1872

One-room schoolhouse built for the community of Rockawalkin. It held grades 1 through 7, later 1 through 5. Located on northeast corner of Maryland Route 349 and Rockawalkin Road, it was abandoned as a school in 1939. Moved to this location, 1973. (16)
Pemberton Road (C0. 70) and Ellegood Street.

❿ Transpeninsular Line
between Maryland and three lower counties of Pennsylvania (now Delaware) - middle point 8 miles

First run 1751. Agreed upon 1760 and finally ratified 1769 by King George III. Thus ending almost a century of controversy between the proprietors of the two provinces. (1)
U.S. 13 and MD 455 at MD - DE State Line.

⓫ Whitehaven
Chartered by Charles Calvert, 3rd Lord Baltimore c. 1685 Town incorporated c. 1702

Ferry operated here as early as 1692. Settlers were led by Colonel George Gale of Whitehaven in the north of England. His first wife, Mildred Warner Washington who by previous marriage was George Washington's Grandmother, lived nearby before her death in 1701. "Whitehaven Company" of Somerset County Militia fought with the Maryland Line in Revolutionary War. (12)
Whitehaven Road (C0. 157) and Church Street.

⓬ Wicomico Presbyterian Church

On March 12, 1672, Somerset County granted Presbyterians permission to conduct regular services on the Wicomico River. The first church, located six miles down river, was one of five churches organized by Francis Mackemie in 1683. It moved to Rockawalkin, 1742, and to Salisbury, 1830. Present sanctuary built, 1859. (4)
North Baptist Street and U.S. 50, Salisbury.

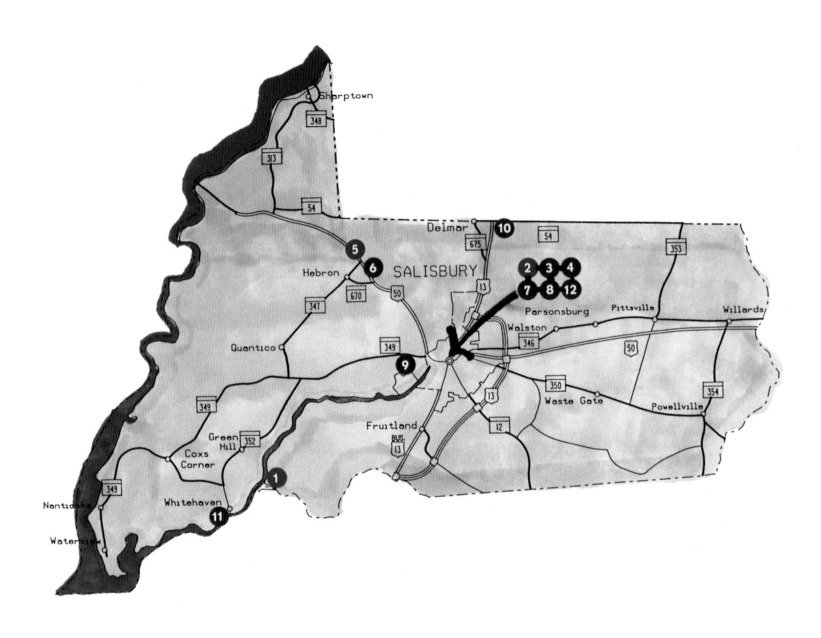

WICOMICO COUNTY

Wicomico County is a transition county between the Chesapeake Bay side of the Eastern Shore and the Atlantic Ocean side which is located in Worcester County. Although there is much industry in Wicomico County the county is filled with rich rural scenery.

WORCESTER COUNTY

 1   Askiminokonson

Indian Town

In 1671 the largest Indian town in Maryland, jointly occupied by the Pokomoke, Annamessex, Manokin, Nassawattex and Acquintica Indians. A large reservation laid out here in 1686.   (1)

MD 12 and MD 354.

2   Boundary Line

Maryland - Virginia

500 feet east of this point near the boundary stone is a large White Gum, one of the old "Marriage Trees" under which Virginia and Maryland couples married.   (1)

MD - VA Line on U.S. 13.

**3   Commodore
Stephen Decatur, USN**

Born near this site January 5, 1779. His heroic exploits in Tripolitan Wars earned him his captain's commission in 1804. Commanded the "United States" and appointed commodore in War of 1812. Killed in duel at Bladensburg, Maryland, March 22, 1820.   (4)

U.S. 113, north of Burley Road.

**4   Eastern End of
Transpenninsular Line**

*between Maryland and three lower
counties of Pennsylvania (now Delaware)
(Fenwick Island)*

First run 1751, agreed upon 1760 and finally ratified 1769 by King George, III, thus ending almost a century of controversy between the proprietors of the two provinces.   (1)

U.S. 113 at MD - DE Line.

5   "Genesar"

*also "Genzar", "Genessar",
"Genezir" and "Genezer"*

2,200 acres "Lying on the sea board side in Boquetonorton (Poqadenorton) Hundred" patented May 10, 1676, to Colonel William Stevens, and on January 10, 1679, to Charles Ratcliffe. Brick house believed built in 1732 by Major John Purnell. During the revolution, Zadok Purnell was authorized to build a battery near here to repel possible attacks from British ships in Sinepuxent Bay.   (5)

South Point Road, 2.4 miles south of MD 611.

 6   Nassawango Iron Furnace

Built 1832 by the Maryland Iron Company to smelt bog iron ore dug from the bed of Nassawango Creek. It was abandon in 1847. The old furnace stack is still standing (1934).   (1)

MD 12 and Old Furnace Road.

7   Old St. Martin's Church

The original Protestant Episcopal Church of Worcester Parish, started 1756, completed 1759 on site of earlier "Chapell"-of - Ease. First Rector, the Reverend Mr. Dingle, and two later Rectors buried under floor of church. Annual service held in June.   (4)

3 miles north of Berlin on U.S. 113.

8   Verrazano Bridge

Named in 1976 for the courageous Florentine navigator, Giovanni Da Verrazano (c. 1485-1528). In the Ship La Dauphine under a commission from King Francis I of France, he explored the Atlantic coastline of North America in the spring of 1524, searching in vain for a route to Asia. In the crew of 50 was his brother, the map maker Girolamo Da Verrazano. Some historians believe the navigator came ashore near here, calling the land Arcadia because of the beauty of the trees.   (14)

West side of MD 611, north end of Bridge.

WORCESTER COUNTY

Worcester County should be called the "Atlantic" county, for it is here that all the ocean front in Maryland is located. The emphasis on Ocean City is probably the reason that Worcester County has the fewest historic markers of any county.

Lower Ocean City

Berlin

Ocean City Life Saving Museum

Snow Hill

LOWER OCEAN CITY - This is one of the great buildings in Old Town or lower Ocean City. These buildings date from the early 1900's. **OCEAN CITY LIFE SAVING MUSEUM** - contains a fabulous collection of historic items used to rescue people from the grips of the ocean. The museum is located at the very bottom of the boardwalk in Ocean City. **BERLIN** - One of the quiet historic gems of Worchester County. **SNOW HILL** - is the county seat of Worchester County. Like Berlin it is full of historic houses.

ORIGINAL STATE HOUSE - ST. MARY'S CITY - Historic St. Mary's City is the oldest settlement in Maryland. It was here that the original state house was built. Pictured above is an exact replica of the original state house in Historic St. Mary's City. It is shown above during the military muster which attracts regiments, who reenact the 1600's, from various states. The weapons they are carrying are match locks and pikes. (See page 95, marker 17)

ST. MARY'S COUNTY

❶ British Landing Prevented
July 17, 1776

Captain Rezin Beall (later Brigadier General in "Flying Camp") was wounded here in repulse of British efforts to cross to mainland from St. George's Island. Fighting continued until July 29. Lord Dunmore, commanding 72 marauding British vessels on Potomac River, was also wounded here. Offshore, five British ships were disabled.   (5)

MD 249, south of St. George Creek Bridge.

❷ Cecil's Mill Historic District

The original water-powered textile mill, "Clifton Factory", built in 1812, was rebuilt as a flour mill in 1900 by John Thomas Cecil. Historic District also includes Cecil's Country Store and Post Office built in 1906.   (54)

MD 5, north of Flat Iron and Indian Bridge Roads.

❸ Chaptico

Established in 1683 as one of the four Ports of Entry in St. Mary's County. Shipping continued until early in the Twentieth Century. Christ Church, built in 1736, has been used continuously since. On July 30, 1814, British Forces looted the Town, causing much damage.   (4)

MD 234 at Chaptico.

❹ Charlotte Hall School

An outgrowth of the "Free Schools" established in Maryland in 1723. Founded in 1774 "to provide for the Liberal and Pious education of the youth of this providence, the better to fit them for the discharge of their duties." Continuously open since 1796.   (1)

MD 5 at Charlotte Hall Road.

❺ "Deep Falls"
Originally patented
March 26, 1680 as "Wales"

Homestead of the Thomas Family. The present house was built in 1745. Major William Thomas Jr. (1758-1813) of the famous "Maryland Line" and Dr. James Thomas (1785-1845) Governor of Maryland 1833-36 lived and lie buried here.   (1)

MD 234, 3 miles west of MD 242.

❻ De La Brooke Manor
Surveyed July 28, 1650

Robert Brooke, First Lord of the Manor, born London, 1602: Died Brooke Place, 1655. Commander of Charles County, 1650. President Provincial Council and Acting Governor of Maryland 1652. Council met at "De La Brooke" 1662. Original manor house destroyed 1835.   (1)

MD 6 and Delabrooke Road.

❼ Erected by the United States

To mark the burial place of Confederate Soldiers and Sailors who died at Point Lookout, Maryland while prisoners of war and were there buried to the number of 3384. But whose remains were subsequently removed either to their respective homes or to this cemetery where the individual graves cannot now be identified.   (51)

MD 5 at Point Lookout State Park.

❽ Fenwick Manor

On April 24, 1651, Cuthbert Fenwick was granted absolute Lordship on Fenwick Manor, sometimes called St. Cuthbert's Manor, with all the rights and privileges of holding Court Baron and Court Leet. The Manor was 2,000 acres in resurrection honored, on the south bank of the Patuxent River. It was between De La Brooke Manor (on the north) and Resurrection Manor (on the south).   (52)

Jones Wharf Road, east of MD 235, north of Hollywood.

Leonardtown
❾ *Established in 1660*

Named Seymour Town in honor of Governor John Seymour and designated St. Mary's County Seat by the Maryland General Assembly in 1708. Name changed to Leonardtown by the General Assembly in 1728 in honor of Leonard Calvert, first Colonial Governor of Maryland.   (4)

North Washington Street and east Fenwick Street

❿ The Manor of
Cornwaleys' Cross

2,000 Acres granted September 8, 1639 to Thomas Cornwaleys who came to Maryland with "The Ark and The Dove". He and Jerome Hawley were appointed "His Lordship's Commissioners for the Government of said Province" 1633 with Leonard Calvert as Governor.   (1)

MD 5, 2.8 miles south of MD 584.

⓫ Mattapany

Site of Jesuit Mission about 1636 on land given by Indian King and called "Mattapanient House". Sacked 1642 by the Indians. Stockaded Fort as Provincial Arsenal there erected. Patented 1663 by Henry Sewell and called "Mattapany-Sewell". His widow married Charles, 3rd Lord Baltimore who lived here 1665. Place of surrender of Proprietary Government August 1, 1689 after which Maryland became a Royal Province until 1715.   (1)

Millstone Road at Patuxent Naval Base.

⓬ Mattapany Street

The first road built by the Colonists in Maryland. It led from "St. Marys" to "Mattapany" on the Patuxent River referred to in 1639 as the "Mattapany Path".   (1)

MD 5 at Mattapany Road.

⓭ Point Lookout
Prisoner-Of-War Camp
1863-1865

After the Battle of Gettysburg, the Union established a prisoner-of-war depot near here. Confederate Soldiers and Maryland Civilians were imprisoned and guarded by 400 Union Troops. With only tents for protection 3,384 prisoners died.   (53)

Point Lookout.

⓮ Saint Clement's Island
(One-half mile offshore)

Site of the first landing of Governor Leonard Calvert and the Maryland Colonists. Andrew White, S. J. celebrated the first Catholic Mass in the British-American Colonies. The island became a part of St. Clement's Manor, granted Dr. Thomas Gerard, November 3, 1639, and later was owned by the Blackstone Family for over two hundred years during which it became known as Blackstone Island.   (4)

Colton's Point, across from St. Clement's Island.

⓯ St. Clement's Island

To this Island in March, 1634, Governor Leonard Calvert and the first Maryland

ST. MARY'S COUNTY

At the very bottom of the Southern Maryland Peninsula is St. Mary's County. It was here that on March 25, 1634, the first English colonists landed. St. Mary's County is full of important historic sites, the center piece of which is Historic St. Mary's City, a reproduction of the original town where Maryland's history began.

Colonist came in the vessels Ark and Dove. Here they took possession of the province of Maryland, erected a cross of Maryland wood and celebrated the Holy Sacrifice. Here they first brought to the new world those principles of religious liberty which have been the chief glory of this state. (4)

Base of commemorative monument, St. Clements Island.

16 St. Joseph's Manor

Nicholas Hervey (also Harvey) having "Prayeth a Grant of a Mannor" of 1,000 acres on south side of Patuxent River in 1641 "for transporting into the province this present year himself, his wife and five other persons," Cecilius Calvert on January 25, 1642 did "will that it be created… by the name of the Mannor of St. Joseph's and have Court Leet and Court Baron with all things thereunto belonging by the law or custome of England." (52)

Town Creek Drive, east of Harbor Lane, California.

17 St. Mary's City
(Capital of Maryland, 1634-1694)

Here, for the first time in America, men and women of different faiths lived in peace and goodwill, practicing freedom of conscience, according to Lord Baltimore's "Instructions to Colonists" 1633. "Freedom Assembled," of various beliefs. Changed practice into law by approving "an act concerning religion," 1649. (4)

MD 5, north of MD 584.

18 St. Mary's Female Seminary

The state's 200th anniversary memorial established by Act of the Legislature of 1839 as a living monument to mark the birthplace of the state and the religious liberty.

MD 584, St. Marys College Grounds.

19 The Three Notch Road

An early law provided that "three notches of equal distance" marked on the trees indicated a road leading to a ferry. "Two notches with another notch a distance above the other two" a road to a court house." A slip cut down the face of a tree near the ground" a road to a church. (1)

Three Notch Road and MD 5.

Historic St. Mary's City

St. Clement's Island

HISTORIC ST. MARY'S CITY - A fabulous restoration of St. Mary's City by the state has recreated much of the feeling of the early 1600's here.
ST. CLEMENT'S ISLAND - It was here on March 25, 1634 that the first colonists landed in Maryland, arriving in the "Ark" and the "Dove".

PORT TOBACCO - located on a tributary of the wide Potomac River, this quiet town was once a thriving port. The original site was the Indian village of Potobac which was visited by Captain John Smith in 1608. Port Tobacco was also visited by George Washington in his trips up and down the East Coast. (See page 99, marker 37; and page 101, markers 40 and 41).

CHARLES COUNTY

1 ## Araby

The widow Eilbeck, mentioned in Washington's diary, lived here. Her daughter, Ann Eilbeck, married Colonel George Mason of Gunston Hall, Virginia. Araby built about 1700. (4)

MD 225, 0.5 mile south of Mason Springs.

2 ## Benedict

Founded in 1683 as Benedict Leonardtown. Here a vessel was constructed for George Washington in 1760. In August, 1814, British Troops under General Ross landed near here for their march on the City of Washington. (1)

MD 231, west of Benedict Avenue.

3 ## Boarman's Manor

3,333 Acres

Granted, 1674, to William Boarman Esquire with royal courts, perquisites, profits of courts and other privileges and immunities belonging to manors in England. By proprietary patent Lord Baltimore granted the prerogatives of Court Baron and all things belonging thereunto. (130)

Catholic Church in Bryantown.

4 ## Booth's Pine Thicket

About a quarter mile to the south, John Wilkes Booth and David Herold remained hidden while Union Troops sought them. Thomas A. Jones brought them food and news of developments. (127)

Location ?

5 ## "Brentland"

2.6 miles

Birthplace of Acting Brigadier General Joseph Lancaster Brent, C.S.A. (1826-1909). He served in the Trans-Mississippi Department during the Civil War and took part in the Siege of Vicksburg. (127)

MD 6 and Cedar Point Neck Road.

6 ## Budd's Ferry

1 mile

Site of a Union Battery, November 1861 to March 1862. The movements of Confederate Troops across the Potomac in Virginia were observed from a balloon above this point. (127)

MD 224, 2 miles south of MD 344.

7 ## Camp Stanton

Was established in this area, October, 1863, for the recruiting and training of the Seventh, Ninth, Nineteenth and Thirtieth United States Colored Infantry. (127)

MD 231, at Benedict Avenue.

8 ## Cedar Point

February, 1766, Washington's schooner ran aground off this point. From his diary of August 25th, 1768, "hauling seine upon the bar off Cedar Point for sheepshead but catched none." (138)

At Morgantown Ferry on road leading to Clubhouse of old amusement park.

9 ## Chandler's Hope

2 miles

Job Chandler, first Charles County settler, built the oldest part of this house, 1639-1650, aided by the Potopaco Indians. Later it was the birthplace of Archbishop Leonard Neale, one of six brothers, all catholic priests, and one sister, a nun. First (temporary) seat of Carmelite Nuns in America, 1790. (4)

U.S. 301 and Stage Coach Road.

10 ## Chapman's Landing

A landing used in crossing to Gunston Hall lying opposite. Washington attempted to cross here in 1786 but roughness of river prevented. (131)

MD 210, 1 mile northeast of MD 225.

11 ## Christ Church Episcopal

Parish church of Port Tobacco Parish. One of the 30 Church of England Parishes established, 1692, by Act of the Provincial Assembly, supported by a yearly poll tax of 40 pounds of tobacco. In 1904 the edifice was moved stone by stone from Port Tobacco and rebuilt on this site. (4)

MD 6 and Church Street, LaPlata.

12 ## Christ Church
William and Mary Parish

1690

Known originally as Piccawaxen. The parish was renamed William and Mary under the Establishment Act of 1692. Christ Church, in existence in 1690, enlarged in 1750, is otherwise unchanged except for post Civil War repairs. The boyhood church of Thomas John Clagett, first Bishop consecrated in the United States (1792). This is the oldest public building in Charles County. (127)

MD 257, north of Morgantown Road.

13 ## Church of St. Joseph

Established in 1763 by
Father Joseph Hunter, S. J.
Maurice McDonough

The 18th Century merchant who died in 1804 is buried here. He willed his modest wealth to establish free schools for the education of poor children in the section of Charles County where he had worked as a peddler and storekeeper for many years. Though his benevolence the McDonough Charity fund was incorporated in 1807. Free schools were established and by 1900 the fund was sufficient to found the first school in the county that offered high school education called "The McDonough Institute". It opened in September 1903 and served the county until 1927. The McDonough Charity fund since then has provided college scholarships for persons residing within the original McDonough District. (127)

MD 227, 0.8 mile east of Pomfret.

14 ## Cliffton

The home of Major Roderick G. Watson is two miles north of this marker. At the start of the Civil War many persons crossed the Potomac River to Virginia in this area. From 1862 to the end of the war, Thomas A. Jones served as a Confederate Agent forwarding mail from the south to the north and Canada. Mary, daughter of Major Watson, hung a signal in a dormer window of Cliffton when it was not safe for the mail boat to cross from Virginia. (127)

U.S. 301, 1.1 mile north of Potomac River Bridge.

15 ## Dent's Meadow

One Mile

John Wilkes Booth and David Herold set out from here for the Virginia shore during the night of April 21, 1865, in a boat supplied by Thomas A. Jones. (127)

Popes Creek Road, 1.8 miles north of Popes Creek.

CHARLES COUNTY

To the north and west of St. Mary's County is Charles County. It is bordered on the west and south by the Potomac River. This is a county full of picturesque farms and fishing piers.

16 ### Dr. Mudd's House

Dr. Mudd set the broken leg of John Wilkes Booth who escaped from Washington after Lincoln's assasination on April 14, 1865. Dr. Mudd was tried and imprisoned on Dry Tortugas Island. (1)

MD 5, 1 mile below Waldorf.

17 ### Durham Church

Durham Parish organized and a log church built in 1692. The present brick church built in 1732. Rebuilt through efforts of General William Smallwood in 1791. (139)

U.S. 301 and MD 6.

18 ### "Efton Hills"

Birthplace of Admiral Raphael Semmes C.S.N. Appointed a Midshipmen U.S.N., 1826, he served in the Mexican War with distinction. Joining the Confederate Navy, 1861, he commanded the noted Confederate Raider the "Alabama". (127)

MD 6, 0.2 mile of MD 425.

19 ### Eutaw

Home of Captain William Fendlay Dement, 1st Maryland Artillery, C.S.A. He served with distinction at Seven Pines, Second Manassas, Cedar Run, Harpers Ferry, Gettysburg, Appomattox and Sharpsburg. Buried at Pomfret. (127)

MD 228, 3 mile north of Pomfret.

20 ### General Daniel E. Sickles, U.S.A.

Commander of the "Excelsoir Brigade", New York Volunteers. Maintained headquarters here October, 1861 to March, 1862. (127)

MD 6, 2 miles southwest of Doncaster.

21 ### General Joseph Hooker, U.S.A.

Maintained headquarters here at Chiccamuxen Methodist Church from October, 1861 to March, 1862, when over 12,000 Union Troops were camped along the Potomac River in Charles County. (127)

MD 224, 1 mile east of MD 344.

22 ### Green Park

Home of Basil Spaulding who enlisted in the Confederate Cavalry at seventeen years of age. He served in the famous unit, Mosby's Partisans. (127)

Location?

23 **Home of Dr. Samuel Mudd**
1833-1883

John Wilkes Booth rested here for several hours on April 15, 1865, after receiving treatment for his broken leg. (127)

MD 232, 0.4 mile south of MD 382.

24 **Home of Dr. Stoughton W. Dent**

Confederate mail carrier from Popes Creek to Bryantown and Charlotte Hall. His son, George, served in the Second Maryland Infantry, CSA. (127)

Near Upper Marlboro.

25 **"Huckleberry"**

Home of Confederate mail agent, Thomas A. Jones, who helped to shelter, and aided the escape of John Wilkes Booth and David Herold in their flight, April 16th to 21st 1865. (127)

Popes Creek Road, 1 mile south of U.S. 301.

26 **Indian Head**

Site of Indian tribes prior to the first settlers. Since 1890, a proving grounds and propellant research center for the United States Navy. (127)

MD 210, south of Poplar Lane.

27 **John Wilkes Booth**

John Wilkes Booth and David Herold crossed into Charles County near this spot after President Abraham Lincoln's assassination on April 14, 1865 . (127)

MD 5 and MD 382.

28 **John Wilkes Booth**

And his accomplice Herold hid in a thick woods on Samuel Cox's Farm (one mile north) for several days before escaping to Virginia after Lincoln's assassination April 14, 1865. (1)

Bel Alton Road (MD 382) at Fairgrounds Road.

29 **John Wilkes Booth and David Herold**

Remained hidden from April 16 to 21, 1865 in a nearby pine thicket, while Union Troops searched for them. Thomas A. Jones brought them food and the news. (127)

Bel Alton Road and Wills Road.

30 **John Wilkes Booth and His Companion David Herold**

Entered Charles County near this spot after assassinating President Lincoln in Washington on April 14, 1865. (127)

U.S. 301, south of Prince George's County Line.

31 **Keechland**

Part of large tract reserved as public land by Cecilius Calvert, Lord Baltimore. Warrant issued 1667 to John Harrison for 600 acres of which 250 assigned to Thomas and Andrew Baker, called Harrison's Gift. Colonel William Dent purchased in 1692. George Dent, his son, enlarged plantation to 1383 acres, naming it Prospect Hill. Seat of Dent family for 200 years. Manor house burned by British in 1781. Present house is 20th century, known as Keechland since 1918. (130)

Popes Creek Road, 1 mile north of Popes Creek.

32 **Laidler's Ferry**

Near present bridge was Laidler's Landing which George Lee deeded to John Laidler in 1760. On main route to Fredericksburg and Williamsburg, it as also called Ledler's and Laidlaw's in George Washington's diary. To the south is Cedar Point, where Washington's schooner ran aground in February, 1766. He wrote in his diary August 25, 1768: "Hauling seine upon the bar off Cedar Point for sheepshead but catched none." (5)

U.S. 301, south of Clifton Drive.

33 **Marshall Hall**

Built by William Marshall in 1690 on land obtained from the Piscataway Indians. Maryland landing of Posey Ferry used by Washington. Mount Vernon in sight from river shore. (137)

MD 227 at entrance to Piscataway Park in Marshall Hall.

34 **Mattawoman Run**
Charles and Prince George's Counties

Named for the Mattawoman Indians who had a fort and town in this locality. In 1670 Governor Charles Calvert presented to their King, Maquata, a medal with the likeness of his father, Cecilius, Second Lord Baltimore, on one side and a map of Maryland on the other. (1)

U.S. 301, south of Prince George's County line.

35 **Milestones in Radio History**

Here, on Cobb Island, in December, 1900, Reginald Aubrey Fessenden, assisted by Frank W. Very, while experimenting in wireless telephony, for the first time sent and received intelligible speech by electromagnetic waves between two masts 50 feet high and one mile apart. (4)

On Cobb Island at Crain and Bridge Boulevards

36 **"The Monastery"**
First Carmel in U.S.

Founded October 15, 1790, by four Carmelites from Belgium, three of them natives of Maryland. Nuns moved to Baltimore September 13, 1831. The restorers of Mount Carmel in Maryland recovered site March 27, 1935. Restored buildings 1937. (1)

Mitchell Road, 1.9 miles southwest of U.S. 301.

37 **Mulberry Grove**

Birthplace of John Hanson, April 14, 1715. President of the United States in Congress assembled 1781-1782. Died Oxon Hill, Maryland, November 22, 1783 . (129)

Chapel Point Road, 1.5 miles south of Port Tobacco.

38 **Myrtle Grove Game Refuge**

800 Acres, purchased May 25, 1929, from Walter J. Mitchell, Attorney for Mortgagee; from Hunter's License Fund, for the purpose of propagating game. (3)

MD 225, 0.5 mile north of Ripley.

39 **Old Durham Church**
Episcopal - 1692

11.9 miles west near Ironsides, Maryland. Oldest church in Charles County. Served by thirty rectors through 257 years. Present building erected 1732. Visited by George Washington 1771. Restored by Governor Smallwood 1791. (133)

U.S. 301 and MD 6.

Dr. Mudd's House

General Smallwood's House

Charles County Farm

CHARLES COUNTY FARM - This Amish Farmer harvests his field much like they have been harvested for hundreds of years. Much of Charles County is still rich farm land. (See page 97, marker 3 and page 101, markers 52, 53, and 54). **DR. MUDD'S HOUSE** - It was in this house that on April 15, 1865 Dr. Mudd set the broken leg of John Wilkes Booth. (See page 98, marker 16 and page 99, marker 23). **GENERAL SMALLWOOD'S HOUSE** - This modest home in what is now a truly magnificent state park was once the home of General William Smallwood. General Smallwood was the commander of the Maryland troops who saved Washington's Army on Long Island. (See page 101, marker 47).

Port Tobacco

In this center of Confederate activity, at the Brawner Hotel, Detective Captain William Williams, unsuccessfully offered Thomas Jones $100,000 reward for information that would lead to the capture of John Wilkes Booth. (127)

In front of the Old Court House in Port Tobacco.

 Port Tobacco

The Indian village of Potobac, visited in 1608 by Captain John Smith, occupied this site. County seat of Charles County, 1658- 1895. Washington visited here frequently. Site of Saint Colombia Lodge No. 11 A.F. and A.M., chartered April 18, 1793. (136)

MD 6, east of Chapel Point Road.

 The Retreat

Daniel St. Thomas Jenifer's home. First President of the Maryland Senate 1777-81. Close friend of George Washington who visited here June 3rd, 1763. (1)

MD 6 and Poor House Road (MD 484).

 Rich Hill

Mid-18th Century farm house (with alterations after 1800) was home of Colonel Samuel Cox. This southern sympathizer fed and sheltered fugitives John Wilkes Booth and David E. Herold before dawn on Easter Sunday, April 16, 1865. Following Booth's assassination of President Abraham Lincoln, Booth and Herold hid in woods until night of April 21, when Cox's foster brother, Thomas A. Jones, helped them escape across the Potomac to Virginia. (4)

Bel Alton-Newton Road, 2 miles east of U.S. 301.

 Rose Hill

Home of Miss Olivia Floyd, Confederate Agent, and her brother Robert Semmes Floyd, C.S.A., killed in action. Both are buried in St. Ignatius Churchyard two miles south. (127)

Rose Hill Road, 0.6 mile north of MD 6.

 Rose Hill

Home of Dr. Gustavus Richard Brown who lies buried here. He was a close friend of George Washington and was one of the

physicians in attendance of his death. (1)

Rose Hill Road, 0.6 mile north of MD 6.

 Rum Point
1 1/2 miles

A landing on Mattawoman Creek used from December, 1861 to March, 1862 to unload supplies for a Brigage of New Jersey Troops encamped nearby. (127)

MD 224, at Stumpneck Road, Marbury.

 Smallwood's Home

One mile from here lived General William Smallwood, Commander of the Maryland Troops which saved Washington's Army at Long Island. Governor of Maryland from 1785 to 1788. Washington visited here in 1786. (132)

MD 224 and Sweden Point Road.

 St. Ignatius Catholic Church, St. Thomas Manor, Chapel Point, Maryland

Dating from 1662 the oldest continuously active parish in the United States. Founded 1641 by Father Andrew White, S.J., who named Chapel Point. Present church built 1798. St. Thomas Manor has been a Jesuit residence since its erection in 1741. (128)

MD 427, 1.8 mile west of U.S. 301.

 St. Mary's Church

In 1700 a frame chapel ministered to by Jesuit Missionaries was attached to the home of Major William Boarman. Father David erected a church in 1793. Under Father Courtney in 1845 a new brick church was begun which is the middle section of the present building. Fire destroyed all but the walls in 1963. The rebuilt church was dedicated in 1966. St. Mary's was established as a separate parish from the Waldorf, Aquasco and Benedict areas in 1851. (127)

MD 232, 1 mile south of Bryan town .

 Surgeon General Revolutionary Army

Dr. James Craik, friend and family physician of General Washington, built this place, La Grange, about 1765 and lived here until his

removal to Alexandria, Virginia. (127)

MD 6, east of Waltnut Hill Road.

 Thomas Stone

Born 1744 - Died 1787 signer of the Declaration of Independence. Member of Congress 1775-1784. One time its presiding officer. He lies buried at his home "Harbor De Venture" one mile south. (135)

MD 225 and Rose Hill Road.

52 Washington's Farm

Two miles southwest Washington owned 600 acres of land bought in 1775 and retained until his death. In 1786 he visited this property accompanied by General Smallwood. (134)

MD 926 (old MD 6) and Liverpool Point Road.

53 Wollaston Manor

2,000 acres patented 1642 to Captain James Neale and named for his Grandfather's home in Northamptonshire, England. Neale's wife, Anne Gill, was Lady-in-Waiting to wife of Charles I, Queen Henrietta Maria. Arriving in Maryland c. 1636, Neale traded with Indians, was member of Privy Council, a Commissioner of Treasury and Magistrate. Four children born while he was King's Emissary to Spain and Portugal. Became Maryland's first naturalized citizens after his return to province in 1660. House built then near here survived to 1900, vas known as "Lone Holly". (130)

At Potomac View, west of MD 257 and Issue.

54 Wolleston Manor
(2000 acres with Court Leet and Court Baron)

Patented in 1642 to Captain James Neale member of the Council and Commissioner of his Lordship's Treasury 1643. House built 1661 (since destroyed) . (1)

U.S. 301 at MD 257.

55 300 Year Old Southern Red Oak
(Circumference 15'7"; Height 72'; Spread 98')

This beautiful tree has been preserved by the Potomac Electric Power Company in cooperation with the Charles County Garden Club October 1965. (157)

MD 257, south of U.S. 301.

DRUM POINT LIGHTHOUSE - Built in 1883 this screw pile lighthouse originally stood 125 yards offshore at the entrance of the Patuxent River leading into the Chesapeake Bay. The lighthouse was decommissioned in 1962 and moved to its present location at the Calvert County Maritime Museum in 1975. (See page 103, marker 12).

CALVERT COUNTY

❶ All Saints Episcopal Church

All Saints, one of the original Parishes of Maryland, included all the land north of Hunting Creek in Calvert County. The present Church was started in 1774 by exchange of Tobacco under the rectorship of Reverend Thomas John Clagett, later the First Bishop consecrated on American soil.   (4)

MD 2/4 on Island in Church Grounds.

❷ Amphibious Training Base

This Nation's first Naval Amphibious Training Base was established here at Solomons where between 1942 and 1945 some 68,000 sailors, marines, coast guardsmen and soldiers were trained. They formed the major components of the Amphibious Forces which landed at Guadalcanal, North Africa, Sicily and Normandy. Ironically, some of those trained here at Solomons, Maryland, participated in the landings in the Solomons Island in the Pacific.   (74)

MD 2/4 and Dowell Road.

❸ Arthur Storer Planetarium

Arthur Storer (c. 1642-1686), the first astronomer in the American Colonies, came to Calvert County from Lincolnshire, England. He was among the first observers to sight and record data describing Halley's Comet on its return in 1682. His observations were made from this tract of land. Arthur Stoner was a lifelong friend and colleague of Sir Isaac Newton who quoted Stoner's data repeatedly in his great scientific works.   (74)

MD 402 and Dares Beach Road, near Prince Frederick.

❹ Battle Creek Cypress Swamp
(2 miles)

A Bald Cypress Reserve and an Amphibian Sanctuary. One of the last remaining stands of Bald Cypress in Maryland, and the most northerly growth in the country. Registered as a Natural Landmark, 1965.   (4)

MD 2/4 and MD 506.

❺ Birthplace of Roger Brooke Taney
1777 - 1864

Member Maryland Senate 1816-21; Attorney General of Maryland 1827-31; Attorney General of the U.S. 1831-33; Secretary of the U.S. Treasury 1833-34; Chief Justice of the U.S. 1836-64; Administered Presidential Oath to Van Buren, Harrison, Polk, Taylor, Pierce, Buchanan and Lincoln.   (1)

MD 765A, 0.2 mile south of MD 231

❻ Brewhouse
Surveyed 1651
5 1/2 miles Mackall's Landing

Birthplace of Thomas Johnson (1732-1819). Member of Continental Congress 1774. Nominated Washington as Commander-in-Chief Continental Army 1775. First elected Governor of Maryland 1777. Associate Justice United States Supreme Court 1791. (4)

MD 2/4, 1 mile south of St. Leonard.

❼ Calvert County

Established as Patuxent County. In 1654, it was given Lord Baltimore's family name in 1658. Now the State's smallest County, it once encompassed most of Prince George's and parts of Anne Arundel and St. Mary's Counties. A narrow peninsula with the "Cliffs of Calvert" on the Chesapeake Bay side. The county slopes gently to the Patuxent River on the west. At the southern tip is the deep-water harbor of Solomons. Although Captain John Smith explored the area in 1608, the county's first permanent settlement was on St. Leonard's Creek c. 1640.   (74)

MD 4 south of County Line.

❽ Chesapeake Beach Railway
1897 - 1935

Built by Otto Mears of Colorado in 1897, the train track linking Washington D.C. to Chesapeake Beach crossed here. The original Depot, to the east, is now the Railroad Museum. Excursion steamboats also brought passengers to Chesapeake Beach from Baltimore. The popular seaside resort and the railroad each depended on the other until the railroad failed in the depression of the 1930's.   (74)

MD 261, 0.5 mile south of MD 260.

❾ Chesapeake Biological Laboratory

Founded by R.V. Truitt, 1928. Sponsored by Maryland Conservation Department since 1931, in cooperation with Carnegie Institution, Johns Hopkins and Maryland Universities, Goucher, St. John's, Washington, and Western Maryland Colleges "to afford a research and study center where facts tending toward a fuller appreciation of nature may be gathered and dissminated. "   (4)

Memorial Drive (Solomons Island).

❿ Christ Church
(Episcopal) 1672

One of the original parishes of the Province of Maryland and Calvert County's oldest continuously worshipping congregation. Christ Church began with a log church standing as early as 1672. Christ Church Parish, 1692, included all the land south of Hunting Creek. The present church dates from 1772.   (4)

MD 264, 0.5 mile south of MD 214, Port Republic.

⓫ The Cliffs of Calvert

First described in 1608 by Captain john Smith and marked on his map. One of the most unusual natural curiosities in the State.
(1)

MD 2/4 at MD 509.

⓬ Drum Point Lighthouse
1883 - 1962

This Lighthouse, installed in 1883, originally stood 125 yards off shore at the entrance of the Patuxent River to the Chesapeake Bay. The foundations on which the cottage-living quarters rest consist of seven wrought iron screw piles, hand bored into the river bottom. The cupola houses a fixed navigational lantern. During fog, a 1,400 pound bell was rung. Decommissioned in 1962, the Lighthouse was moved to the Calvert Marine Museum in 1975.   (74)

Solomon's Island Road, south of MD 2/4.

⓭ Early Settlements

Town of St. Leonard was originally, in 1683, at mouth of St. Leonard Creek. By 1706, when chartered by Maryland General Assembly as a Port of Entry, it had been moved to head of creek near here. British Forces burned its wharves and warehouses July 4, 1814. After 1900, town gradually shifted to its present location 3 miles north.   (75)

MD 2/4 north of MD 765 near St. Leonard.

⓮ J.C. Lore & Sons Oyster House

Joseph C. Lore, Sr., began shipping seafood from Solomons Island in 1888 and established a packing house at this site in 1912.

CALVERT COUNTY

Calvert County is a large county which stretches from Anne Arundel County in the north to St. Mary's County in the south. It is situated between the Chesapeake Bay and the Patuxent River in the west. It is rich in scenic beauty, historic sites, small inlets, and beaches.

Three generations of Lore family packed and shipped Patuxent River oysters, crabs and fish until 1978. Present building dates from 1934, replacing earlier one destroyed in 1933 storm, and is built on oyster shells discarded by Lore Company and neighboring H.M. Woodburn Company, (1918-1943). Lore Oyster House building purchased in 1980 by Calvert Marine Museum. (74)

MD 2, Solomons Island.

15 Joseph & James Wilkinson
(Two Revolutionary Leaders who grew up on farm south of Hunting Creek)

Joseph Wilkinson was Colonel in the Revolution and a Legislator. His younger brother James, an adventurer, first attained General's rank in 1777 at the age of 20. James built a grist mill nearby, became General-in-Chief of Army, was Military Governor of Louisiana Territory 1805-07. Was implicated but acquitted in allegations against Aaron Burr. Both Wilkinson's served as Generals in the War of 1812. Joseph died in 1820, is buried in family graveyard about 3 1/2 miles west of here. James, who died in 1825, is buried in Mexico. (5)

Stoakley Road, west of MD 2/4, north of Prince Frederick.

16 Middleham Chapel
Founded, 1684, as a Chapel of Ease in Christ Church Parish and named for Middleham, Yorkshire, England. The site has been used for worship since the founding, but the Chapel was rebuilt in 1748. The bell, given by John Holdsworth, is dated 1699. (4)

MD 2/4 north of MD 497.

17 Morgan Hill Farm
The tract, originally known as Morgan's Fresh, was granted, 1651, to Phillip Morgan, a captain in the Puritan Militia. The house, which overlooks St. Leonard Creek, was built before 1670 and served as a lookout station in the War of 1812 and the Civil War. (4)

1 mile east of Lusby on St. Leonard Creek.

18 M. M. Davis Shipyard
1885 - 1974

1885 Marcellus M. Davis established his shipyard at this location. In 1913 the yard was moved to larger quarters across the harbor on Mill Creek. During the 1930's, Davis' yard produced many outstanding wooden yachts which brought International Fame to

Solomons. The "High Tide" won nearly every race she entered until she was handicapped so heavily her owner, Eugene Dupont, refused to race or sell her. The Davis-built Maitou (President Kennedy's yacht one summer) won several Mackinac Straits Races until defeated by "White Cloud" another Davis-built yacht. (74)

MD 2, Solomons Island.

19 One-Room School
1870 - 1932

Port Republic School No. 7 was built about 1870 and closed in 1932. One teacher usually taught seven grades of children who walked as far as three miles to school. Enrollment averaged about 30 pupils in each school. 59 similar schools existed throughout Calvert County. This school was restored by the Calvert Retired Teachers Association in 1977. (74)

MD 264 southwest of MD 2/4.

20 "Preston Cliffs" or "Charles' Gift"
Cecil Calvert, Second Lord Baltimore on March 10, 1658, issued a grant of 1,000 acres on the west side of the Chesapeake Bay to Richard Preston. On May 26, 1967 the land was purchased for the site of the first nuclear power plant in Maryland. (4)

MD 2/4 south of White Sands Road.

21 Preston on Patuxent
Home of Richard Preston, Commander of the North Bank of the Patuxent River, 1649. The Seat of the Puritan Government of Maryland where the Colonial Records were kept 1653-1657. (1)

MD 2/4 and MD 112, St. Leonard.

22 Prince Frederick Library "Firsts"
The west wing of the Library was built in 1903 on Main Street as the County's first bank. In 1913, it was replaced, moved and became the County's first Library; 1916 County's first Boy Scout Troop met there; 1921 it was Prince Frederick's first High School; 1959 it was reorganized as a publicly supported Library and in 1961 was moved to present location. That west wing is known as the Duke Room for Judge William W. Duke who founded the 1913 Library and was Scoutmaster of the First Troop. (74)

Duke Street at Public Library, Prince Frederick.

23 Smithville United Methodist Church
The brick Church, dedicated in 1840, is the oldest standing Methodist Church in Calvert County. The Calvert Circuit began in 1781 with services in homes. By 1789 this circuit had the largest membership in the United States. Fielder B. Smith gave land for this church. Other congregation members gave clay, baked the bricks, and provided much of the interior woodwork. In 1882, the Smithville Circuit of three Churches was formed. In 1980 Smithville became a separated Church. (74)

Ferry Landing west of MD 4.

24 Solomon's Island
Originally called Bourne's (1680). Then Somervell's Island (1740). It became known as Solomon's Island (1867) because of Isaac Solomon's oyster packing facilities here. Shipyards developed to supply the Island's fishing fleet. The famed "Bugeye" sailing craft were built here in the 19th century. The deep, protected harbor has been a busy marine center ever since. In the War of 1812, Commander Joshua Barney's Flotilla sailed from here to attack British Vessels on Chesapeake Bay. The causeway connecting island to mainland was built c. 1870. (75)

MD 2, Solomons Island.

25 St. Leonard Creek
(Scene of Naval Battles during War of 1812)

In June, 1814, Maryland's Commodore Joshua Barney commanded American Flotilla of barges, gunboats and a sloop in attacks on superior British Forces in Patuxent River and its tributary, St. Leonard Creek. After Flotilla moved up Patuxent and was blockaded, British destroyed town of St. Leonard, then located near here at head of creek, before proceeding to Washington, which they burned August 24. (75)

MD 214 south of MD 765 near St. Leonard.

26 Veitch's Cove
James Veitch, born 1628 in Roxburghshire, Scotland. Settled at Veitch's Cove, later known as Veitch's Rest, an original Land Patent granted by Lord Baltimore in 1649. Sheriff of Calvert County 1653-1657. Died 1685. (4)

MD 264 and MD 265.

CARROLL COUNTY FARM MUSEUM - Originally the "Poor House" of Carroll County, this house and farm has become a fabulous collection of objects representing farm life in the 1800's. Pictured above is one of the original post office wagons which began the first rural free delivery service in Carroll County and the country. (See page 107, marker 5).

CARROLL COUNTY

1 **Birthplace of Francis Scott Key Terra Rubra Farm**

Birthplace August 3, 1789. Erected by the Patriotic Order Sons of America and the Pupils of the Public Schools June 12, 1915. Terra Rubra Farm birthplace and early home of the author of the Star Spangled Banner who died in Baltimore, January 11, 1843. (73)

Brucevill Road, 1 mile south of Keysville.

2 **Birthplace of William Henry Rinehart**
1825 - 1874

Sculptor - He began his studies in Baltimore and in 1858 established a studio in Rome. Among his more important works are the Monument to Chief Justice Taney in Annapolis and the completion of the Bronze Doors to the Capitol in Washington. Died in Rome 1874. (1)

On Quaker Hill Road (MD 75), east of Union Bridge.

3 **Bridgeport**

As part of General Meade's screen for Washington as the Confederates invaded Maryland and Pennsylvania, the Third Corps, Army of the Potomac, arrived here June 30, 1863, from Taneytown. Next day General Daniel E. Stickles marched this Corps to Emmitsburg. (7)

MD 140, east of Bullfrog Road, north of Taneytown.

4 **Corbit's Charge**

Here. June 29, 1863, Captain Charles Corbit led Companies C and D, first Delaware Calvary, against General J. E. B. Stuart's Calvary Division. Though repelled by overwhelming force, the attack delayed Stuart, and was a factor in his failure to reach Gettysburg Battlefield before July 2. (72)

Main and Washington Streets, Westminster.

5 **The First Complete County Rural Free Delivery Service**

In the United States was inaugurated by the Post Office Department on December 20, 1899 covering the whole of Carroll County and small parts of adjacent counties with Westminster as the central distributing point. (1)

Main Street (MD 32) and Longwell Avenue, Westminster.

6 **The First Reaping Machine**

In the world was invented by Jacob R. Thomas and tried near this spot in 1811. Obed Hussey perfected and patented the invention in 1839 one year prior to the McCormick Reaper. (1)

MD 75 near Linwood.

7 **German Church - 1760**

Near here was located a place of worship described as the "Evangelical Lutheran and, according to God's Word, reformed, and on both sides Protestant congregation called the German Churche." Continuous worship for 200 years on this site marks it as one of the oldest religious centers in Carroll County. (4)

MD 30, north at Manchester City Limits.

8 **Headquarters Second Corps, Army of the Potomac**

On and about the nearby Babylon Farm Major General Winfield Scott Hancock rested his Corps June 29, 1863. On July 1, the Corps marched through Taneytown to take part in the Battle of Gettysburg. (71)

Union Road, 0.5 mile east of Uniontown.

9 **Hood's Mill**

Near here the Confederate Cavalry of Major General J. E. B. Stuart entered Carroll County from Cooksville about daybreak June 29, 1863. After damaging the tracks and bridge of the B&O Railroad at Sykesville, they marched to Westminster and Gettysburg. (71)

MD 97, 0.5 mile south of Eden Mill Road.

10 **Manchester**

The Second Cavalry Division and the Sixth Corps, Army of the Potomac, camped about Manchester June 30, 1863. Headquarters for Major General John Sedwick was located on nearby Old Fort School House Road. On the night of July 1, the Corps left Manchester and went into battle at Gettysburg the next day. (71)

MD 30 and Westminster - York Streets, Manchester.

11 **Meades Headquarters**

Major General George S. Meade, Commander of the Army of the Potomac, maintained headquarters on the nearby Shunk Farm from June 30 until the night of July 1, 1863. From there he directed the initial concentration of the Union forces at Gettysburg. (4)

MD 194, 1 mile north of Taneytown.

12 **"Pipe Creek Meeting"**

About 1735 William Farquhar and Ann his wife held a Friends (Quaker) meeting at his house. In 1771 he deeded two acres of land on which the meeting house and burying ground are located. Ex-President Hoover's ancestors were members of this meeting. (1)

Quaker Hill Drive, 2 miles south of Ladiesburg Road, Union Bridge.

13 **Robert Strawbridge**

The first preacher of Methodist in America. He formed at his house (still standing, 1938) one-half mile east of here the first class and the first society of American Methodism. He built the first log meeting house (1764) for Methodists in America (Marston Road). (1)

MD 31 at Wakefield Valley Road, west of New Windsor.

14 **Spring Garden**

Christopher Vaughn laid out the town of Hampstead in 1786 on land called Spring Garden, located along the Indian Path from Patapsco (Baltimore) to Letort's Springs (Carlisle) which had been marked by Christopher Gist and made a public road in 1738. (4)

MD 30 and Black Rock Road, Hamstead.

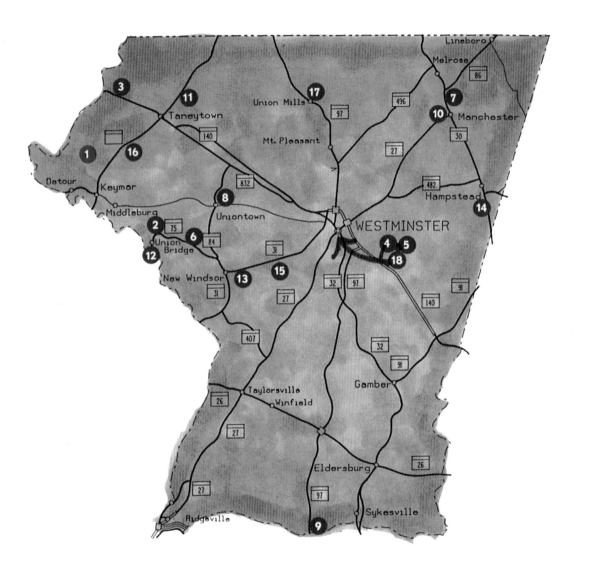

15 Strawbridge Log Meeting House Site

Built in 1764 by Robert Strawbridge. The first Methodist place of worship erected in America. Successors are Stone Chapel (1783) 3 miles northeast, and Bethel (1821) 1 mile south. (70)

MD 407, 0.4 mile south of MD 31.

16 "Terra Rubra"

The birthplace of Francis Scott Key the author of our National Anthem "The Star-Spangled Banner". (4)

MD 194 and Keysville-Bruceville Road.

17 Union Mills

(Built 1797 on the site of an earlier mill by Andrew and David Shriver Jr.)

On June 29, 1863 General J. E. B. Stuart and his Cavalry camped here. On June 30, 1863 General James Barnes of the 5th Corps, U.S. Army spent the night on his way to Gettysburg. (1)

MD 97, north of Deep Run Road.

18 Westminster

County seat of Carroll County, founded 1764. First called Winchester for it's founder William Winchester (1710-1790) who was born in Westminster, England (now part of Greater London). Westminster Academy incorporated 1839 (later absorbed into the public school system). West Maryland College chartered 1868. Confederate Forces under Major Harry Gilmor and General Bradley T. Johnson raided the town in 1864. Union Forces to and from Gettysburg camped here. (1)

MD 140 and MD 559.

CARROLL COUNTY

To the west of Baltimore County, Carroll County is a transision county on the threshold of Western Maryland. The "atmosphere" of the county is mostly rural, yet the county is beginning to be a suburban area for both Washington, D.C. and Baltimore.

Terra Rubra Farm

New Windsor - Farm

Uniontown

NEW WINDSOR - This quiet farm town was the birth place of the Methodist Church in America led by Pastor Robert Strawbridge. (See page 107, marker 13). **TERRA RUBRA FARM** - On August 3, 1789 Francis Scott Key was born on this farm (see page 107, marker 1 and page 108, marker 16). **UNIONTOWN** - This quiet little town was for a brief moment during the Civil War the Headquarters for the Second Corp, Army of the Potomac (see page 107, marker 8).

Hessian Barracks

St. Elizabeth Ann Seton

Roddy Road Covered Bridge

RODDY ROAD COVERED BRIDGE - Frederick County has more covered bridges still in existence from the 1800's than any other county in Maryland. **ST. ELIZABETH ANN SETON** - This woman was responsible for organizing the first Roman Catholic Parochial School in the United States. She was canonized a saint by Pope Paul VI on September 14, 1975. (See page 113, marker 30). **HESSIAN BARRACKS** - Have seen much history since they were the quarters for the Hessian prisons during the Revolutionary War. They were visited by General Lafayette and were used as the staging area by the Lewis and Clark Expedition. (See page 113, marker 20 and 21).

FREDERICK COUNTY

① Amelung Glass Works

First glass manufactory in Maryland. Established by John Frederick Amelung of Bremen, Germany in 1789. George Washington wrote enthusiastically about it to Thomas Jefferson. (1)

MD 355 and Park Mill Road.

② Barbara Fritchie House

Here lived Barbara Fritchie, John Greenleaf Whittier's heroine. The thrilling episode narrated in Whittier's Poem occurred when Stonewall Jackson was on his way through Frederick on September 10, 1862. (4)

MD 144 (Patrick Street), east of Bentz Street, Frederick.

③ The Battle of Monocacy

July 9, 1864

On the banks of the river two miles east of this sign, the Battle of Monocacy was fought between Union Forces under General Lew Wallace, and Confederates under General Jubal A. Early. (4)

U.S. 15 and MD 355.

④ Battle of Monocacy

The Battle that Saved Washington

Here along the Monocacy River on July 9, 1864, was fought the battle between Union Forces under General Lew Wallace and Confederate Forces under General Jubal A. Early. The Battle, although a temporary victory for the Confederates, delayed their march on Washington one day, thereby enabling General Grant to send veteran reinforcements from Petersburg, Virginia, to the defenses of Washington in time forestall the attack by the Confederates and thus save the Capital from capture. (7)

MD 355, 0.5 mile north of the Monocacy River.

⑤ Carroll's Mill

Stone structure nearby was flour mill built in 1812 by Charles Carroll of Carrollton (1737-1832), wealthy landowner and signer of the Declaration of Independence. Site was within his 17,000 acre wilderness tract called "Carrollton Manor". He deeded the mill to Sarah Ann Hoffman in 1821, and subsequent

owners named Doub, Copeland and Smith. (5)

Corner of Pleasant View and Doubs Roads.

⑥ "Carrollton"

Patented for 10,000 acres to Charles and Daniel Carroll, Mary and Ellinor Carroll, 1st April 1724. It was from this tract that Charles Carroll assumed the title "Charles Carroll of Carrollton" when signing the Declaration of Independence . (1)

MD 85, south of Manor Wood Road, Buckeystown.

⑦ Catoctin Furnace

An important iron furnace during the Revolution owned by Governor Thomas Johnson and his brothers. Furnished 100 tons of shells used at Yorktown . (1)

MD 806, 1 mile north of Blacks Mill Road, Catoctin Furnace.

⑧ "Crampton Gap"

An important part of the Battle of South Mountain took place at this Gap September 14-15, 1862, when the Federal Forces pressed back the Confederate Troops into Pleasant Valley and to Sharpsburg. (1)

MD 17 and U.S. 340.

⑨ Forest of Needwood

Estate of Governor Thomas Sim Lee
1745 - 1819

Member Maryland Convention 1775; signer Association of Freedom, Governor of Maryland 1779-1782, 1792-1794; Delegate Continental Congress 1783-1784; member State Convention which ratified the Constitution, 1788. (1)

MD 17 and Lee's Lane.

⑩ Fox's Gap

Elements of D.H. Hill's Division held this pass against the U.S. IX Corps in the Battle of South Mountains, September 14, 1862. In this, Lee's successful delaying action, Major General Jesse Reno, U.S.A. and Brigadier General Samuel Garland, C.S.A. were killed. (7)

Reno Monument Road, near Washington County Line.

⑪ Francis Scott Key

Author of "The Star Spangled Banner"

Born in Frederick County, Maryland, 1779. Died in Baltimore 1843 and there buried. Removed to Frederick 1866 and interred in family lot. In 1898 the remains of Francis Scott Key and Mary Tayloe Lloyd Key, his wife, were placed within the crypt in the base of the monument erected by the Key Museum Association of Frederick, Maryland.

Thomas Johnson

First Governor of Maryland and a nationally known personage during Revolutionary Days, lies buried immediately west of the lot where in lie the remains of Barbara Fritchie.

Barbara Fritchie

A granite shaft on a triangular mound in the southwestern section of the cemetery marks the grave of the heroine of John Greenleaf Whittier's poem. (62)

MD 355, 0.3 mile south of MD 144 in Mt. Olivet Cemetery. (Tablet at entrance).

⑫ General Anthony Wayne

In May and June 1781 marched with his Pennsylvania troops from York, Pennsylvania through Frederick and over this road to Nowland's Ferry where he crossed into Virginia to join Lafayette near Richmond to engage Cornwallis. (1)

U.S. 15 at Point of Rocks Junction.

⑬ General Edward Braddock

Traveled over this road in April 1755 (in a coach and six horses purchased from Governor Horiato Sharpe of Maryland) after a protracted conference in Frederick with Benjamin Franklin and others concerning the securing of teams, wagons and supplies for the expedition against Fort Duquesne. (1)

U.S. 40, 1 mile west of Frederick.

⑭ George Washington

On August 5 and 6, 1785, and again June 30 and July 1, 1791, was the guest of Thomas Johnson at the latter's Manorial Residence,

FREDERICK COUNTY

In Frederick County the mountains of Western Maryland begin in ernest. It is a rather large county which stretches from Pennsylvania to the Potomac River and Virginia. It is full of waterfalls, forests, state, and national parks, and has more covered bridges than any other county in Maryland.

which stood on the site of the present farm house, about 150 yards east of this point. Thomas Johnson, a member of the Continental Congress from Maryland, on June 15, 1775 nominated Washington for Commander in-Chief of the Continental Army. Johnson later became the first Governor of Maryland. (61)

U.S. 15, south of Willow Road.

15 George Washington

On his way to Frederick Friday, August 5, 1785 dined in a building on this site known as The Dutchman's. One mile south of here is Noland's Ferry frequently used by Washington on his travels. (68)

U.S. 15, 3 miles south of MD 26, near Licksville.

16 George Washington

On his way to Philadelphia Friday July 1, 1791 stopped in this building known as Cookerly's Tavern. (65)

MD 194, south of the railroad tracks in New Midway.

17 George Washington

Stopped in a building two hundred yards west of here, known as Peter's Tavern Thursday, June 30, 1791. (66)

MD 355 near Bennett's Run.

18 George Washington

Stopped Thursday, June 30, 1791 in a building on this site known as Colonel Henry Brothers Tavern. (61)

Corner of Patrick and Church Streets, Frederick.

19 Headquarters of General R.E. Lee, "Stonewall" Jackson and Longstreet

September 6 - 9, 1862

Here was written the famous order no. 191 and the proclamation to the people of Maryland. (1)

MD 355, north of Monocacy Battlefield.

20 ## Hessian Barracks
Witness to History

1777 built at direction of Maryland General Assembly; 1778-1779 quartered Hessian and convention prisoners captured at Bennington and Saratoga; 1782 quartered Hessian and Bayreuth Yager Regiments following Cornwallis' surrender; 1799 quartered French Sailors of the L'Insurgent captured by U.S.S. Constellation; 1802-03 served as staging center for Lewis and Clark Expedition; 1812 quartered U.S. Troops during War of 1812; 1824 visited by General Lafayette; 1840-1842 used as silk worm cocoonery; 1853-1860 used for Frederick County Agricultural Society Fairs; 1861-65 housed wounded Confederate and Union Troops; 1868 became Maryland School for the Deaf.   (63)
Clarke Place and Carroll Street on grounds of school, Frederick (Plaque on building).

21 *(Hessian Barracks)*
1776 - 1814
These Barracks mark the course of the struggle for the American Independence

Built in 1777 by the British and Hessian Prisoners of the Revolutionary War. Here were detained those taken at the Battles of Saratoga, Trenton and Yorktown. Also the French Prisoners captured from the frigate "L'Insurgent" by the United States Frigate "Constellation" the first capture of the Navy in 1799. Also the British Prisoners taken in the War of 1812 at Bladensburg, and during the attack upon Baltimore at North Point and Fort McHenry, September 12-14, 1814. The gallant defense of which inspired Francis Scott Key to write the American National Anthem "The Star-Spangled Banner".   (159)
Clarke Place and Carroll Street on grounds of school, Frederick (Plaque on building).

22 ## House of Chief Justice Taney

This house with slave quarters in the rear, was owned by Roger Brooke Taney until the year 1823, when he moved to Baltimore. Taney, Chief Justice of the United States from 1836 to 1864, delivered the opinion in the Dred Scott Case.   (65)
North Bentz Street north of MD 144, Frederick.

23 ## In April 1861
The Legislature of Maryland met here in special session

At this assembly a bill regarded as equivalent to an Ordinance of Secession from the Union was introduced but failed of passage.   (64)
Side of building on Marlet and Church Streets, Frederick.

24 ## J.E.B. Stuart's Ball

The house where General Stuart's dance was held. In the house, for sometime a school for girls, near Peter Pan Inn, General J.E.B. Stuart and other officers of the Confederate Calvary held a dance in September, 1862. The dance was interrupted by a skirmish some miles away.   (4)
MD 355 and MD 80.

25 ## Lewistown Trout Hatchery & Bass Ponds
Frederick County

One mile from this point. Purchased by State 1917.   (2)
U.S. 15 near Lewistown.

26 ## Major General Edward Braddock
1695 - 1755 British Commander, French and Indian War

By coach and six horses purchased from Governor Horatio Sharpe of Maryland, Braddock traveled this route west in April, 1755, after 10-day meeting in Frederick with Benjamin Franklin and others to arrange for teams, wagons and supplies for the expedition against the French at Fort Duquesne. Braddock was mortally wounded 7 miles from that Fort (now Pittsburgh) on July 9, 1755.   (12)
U.S. 40, west of U.S. 15 on State Police Grounds.

27 ## Middletown in the Civil War

September, 1862, soldiers wounded in the Battle of South Mountain were hospitalized in churches here. July 1863, General Meade established headquarters here as Union Forces pursued Confederates retreating from Gettysburg. July, 1864, Confederate General Early occupied Middletown and collected a $1,500 ransom.   (7)
Middletown.

28 ## Reno Monument

Two miles to the southeast stands the monument to Major General Jesse L. Reno who was mortally wounded at the close of the fighting for Fox's Gap in the Battle of South Mountain, September 14, 1862.   (7)
Bolivar on Old U.S. 40.

29 ## Site of St. Joseph's College

On this site St. Elizabeth Ann Seton, the first U.S. native to be canonized, founded an academy for girls in 1809. A high school was later added and in 1902, St. Joseph's College was chartered as a three year institution for women. In 1914 the college was recognized as a four year college empowered to award degrees in the Arts and Sciences. It closed in 1973. The Alumnae Association founded in 1897 is still active.   (69)
333 South Seton Avenue, Emmitsburg.

30 ## St. Elizabeth Ann Seton
Founder of the Sisters of Charity

Born August 28, 1774, in New York, she came to Emmitsburg from Baltimore June 24, 1809, occupying stone house on these grounds July 31. The following year, in white house visible from here, she organized Nation's first Roman Catholic Parochial School. After her death January 4, 1821, she was buried in "The Little Wood". In 1846 her body was reinterred in Mortuary Chapel. Canonized a Saint by Pope Paul VI September 14, 1975. She is first native of United States so honored.   (67)
South Seton Avenue, Emmitsburg.

31 ## Sugar Loaf Mountain

So called in 1710 by a Swiss Nobleman, Baron Graffenried who ascended it in search of silver mines with Martin Chartier, a remarkable Frenchman, married to a Shawnee Indian wife, who lived near the mouth of the Monocacy River.   (1)
MD 28 and Ephren Road, just north of B&O Bridge, Dickerson.

ANTIETAM NATIONAL BATTLEFIELD - It is hard to believe that Washington County with all its beauty was the site of the battle at Antietam. In this battle more men lost their lives in a single day of battle than any in the history of our nation. Each year, in December, The Illumination at Antietam honors the 23,000 plus men who were killed, wounded or missing in the battle on September 17, 1862. (See page 115, markers 1, 3, 4, 7, 8, 11, 12, 13, and 14).

WASHINGTON COUNTY

❶ Antietam Battlefield

12 miles to Antietam National Battlefield site where, on September 17, 1862, about 41,000 Confederates under the command of General Robert E. Lee were pitted against 87,000 Federals under General George B. McClellan. (49)

MD 65 in Hagerstown.

❷ "The Bank Road"
The Cumberland Turnpike Road

The portion of this highway from the west end of the Conococheague Bridge to Cumberland (40 miles) was built between 1816 and 1821. The banks of Maryland financed it by purchase of the stock. (1)

U.S. 40, west of Conococheague Creek.

❸ The Battle of Antietam or Sharpsburg

The bloodiest conflict of the war between the States occurred September 17, 1862, a few miles from this point (turn in the center of Boonsboro). (1)

Alt. U.S. 40, west of MD 67.

❹ The Battle of Antietam or Sharpsburg

Three miles northeast of this point lies Sharpsburg, Maryland, the scene of the bloodiest conflict of the war between the States, occurring September 17, 1862. (47)

Rumsey Bridge on MD 34.

❺ Battle of Funkstown
July 10, 1863

General J. E. B. Stuart protecting Lee's retreat from Gettysburg engaged Union Troops under General Buford here. Day long battle resulted in 479 men killed and wounded. (1)

U.S. 40A in Funkstown.

❻ Battle of Funkstown
July 10, 1863

After Gettysburg, in order to mask entrenching operations along the Potomac River by General R. E. Lee, Confederate Troops, led by General J. E. B. Stuart, engaged Union Forces under General John Buford. The day-long battle east of the road resulted in 479 casualties. The Chaney House served as a hospital and at the Keller Home Major H. D. McDaniel, later Governor of Georgia, survived wounds. (4)

U.S. 40A in Funkstown.

❼ Blackford's Ford

Also known as Boteler's, Pack Horse and Shepherdstown Ford. "Stonewall" Jackson's Command crossed here en route from Harper's Ferry to Sharpsburg. Here the entire Army of Northern Virginia withdrew into Virginia, September 18-19, 1862 following the Battle of Antietam. (7)

MD 34 near Rumsey Bridge and "Ferry Hill" sign.

❽ Brownsville - Burkettsville Pass

Marching from Middletown to seize Maryland Heights, McLaw's and Andersons' Confederate Divisions crossed South Mountain by this road September 11, 1862. On September 14th Manly's North Carolina Battery and elements of Semmes' Brigade defended the pass and protected Howell Cobb's right flank. (7)

MD 67 in front of Brownsville Post Office.

❾ Chaney House
used as Civil War Hospital

In Battle of Funkstown, July 10, 1863 this house was used as hospital. Surgeons operated on lawn under trees. In the evening, Mr. Chaney's negro slaves sang spirituals for the dying. (4)

U.S. 40A in Funkstown.

❿ Colonel Nathaniel Rochester
(1752 -1831)

Who founded the City of Rochester, New York lived in Hagerstown 1783-1810 was Postmaster, Judge of the County Court and member of the Maryland Assembly. Founded the Hagerstown Bank and in partnership with Colonel Hart manufactured flour, rope and nails here. (1)

Alt. U.S. 40, south of Wilson Boulevard at Kenly Avenue.

⓫ Confederate Retreat

Driven from Campton's Gap on September 14, 1862 by General Franklin's Sixth Corps, elements of McLaw's Confederates formed across Pleasant Valley to bar Union advance on Maryland Heights and Harpers Ferry. Later these Confederates joined Lee about Sharpsburg. (7)

Gapland Road at MD 67.

⓬ Confederate Trenches

Manning the trenches just before you Lee's Troops on September 14, 1862, fought to hold Crampton's Gap against McClellan's Union Army advancing up South Mountain from the Middletown Valley below. At sunset the Confederates were overwhelmed but the delaying action made possible the capture of Harper's Ferry by other Southern Forces thus paving the way to the bloody Battle of Antietam three days later. (50)

Gathland State Park near "Gath" Mansion on South Mountain.

⓭ Crampton Gap

An important part of the Battle of South Mountain was fought here September 14-15, 1862, when the Federal Forces pressed the Confederate Troops back into Pleasant Valley and on to Sharpsburg. (1)

MD 67 at Gapland Road.

⓮ "Crampton's Gap" "Maryland Heights" and "Pleasant Valley"

Important points during the first invasion of Maryland by the Army of the Confederacy in 1862. (1)

Alt. U.S. 40, east of MD 67.

⓯ Cushwa Trout Rearing Station
Washington County

Two miles from this point. (2)

Old U.S. 40 between Hagerstown and Hancock.

⓰ Falling Waters

Retreating after Gettysburg the Confederate Army was trapped for seven days by the swollen Potomac River. July 13th-14th General Lee with Longstreet's and Hill's crossed here on a pontoon bridge. Eweil's Corps forded the Potomac above Williamsport. (7)

Falling Waters Road and C & O Canal.

WASHINGTON COUNTY

Washington County, named after our first president, is located west of Frederick County. The Appalachian Trail crosses Maryland in Washington County. The county is filled with farms, picturesque mountains, valleys, and streams. One of the most visited historic sites in the state is the Civil War Battlefield of Antietam.

The Federal Sign Station

Near this point was captured October 10, 1862 by a detachment of General J. E. B. Stuart's Calvary. On clear days this station could communicate with stations on South Mountain which relayed messages via Catoctin Mountain to Sugarloaf Mountain to Washington D.C.   (1)

U.S. 40 on Fairview Mountain.

 Ferry Hill Place

(Built in 1812)

The boyhood home of Colonel Henry Kyd Douglas. A member of Stonewall Jackson's Staff. September 18, 1862, Federal Troops occupied these premises and confined the Douglas Family. June 18, 1863, headquarters Confederate Major General Edward Johnson en route to Pennsylvania.   (7)

MD 34 near Rumsey Bridge.

19 Fort Coombe

A Maryland stockaded fort of 1755-56 located north of this point. One of the frontier forts during the French and Indian War. The survey of the Mason and Dixon Line during 1763-68 placed it in Pennsylvania instead of Maryland.   (1)

High Street and Jackson Street in Hancock.

20 Fort Frederick

Maryland State Park

Colonial stone fort built 1756 for Province of Maryland by Governor Horatio Sharpe to protect frontier against French and Indians after Braddock's defeat. Detention camp for British prisoners 1776-83. Occupied 1861-62 by Union Troops. George Washington was here July 1756 and June 1758.   (1)

U.S. 40, east of MD 56.

U.S. 40 and Martin Street, Clear Spring

21 Fort Mills

One of the four stockade forts erected in 1756 along the North Mountain Road as supports for Fort Frederick in preventing the Indians from descending upon the inhabitants living in the Cumberland Valley.   (1)

U.S. 40, west of exit 9 from I-70 at Licking Creek.

22 General Edward Braddock

In April 1755 (driven in his coach and six

horses) crossed into Virginia near this point on his way to Fort Cumberland. After ten days' conference with Benjamin Franklin and others in Frederick, Maryland, arranging for teams and supplies for the expedition to Fort Duquesne.   (1)

MD 34, Main Street and Big Springs Avenue, Sharpsburg.

 General J. E. B. Stuart

With General Wade Hampton attacked a large force of Pennsylvania Militia under Governor Curtin and General John F. Reynolds near here September 20, 1862. Outnumbered he retired across the Potomac. He desired to seize federal supplies at Hagerstown.   (1)

U.S. 11 between Tammany Lane and Sheridan Drive.

 General J. E. B. Stuart's

Calvary on his raid around the Federal Army, October 10, 1862, crossed the National Road here after crossing the Potomac River at McCoy's Ferry three miles south of this point.   (1)

U.S. 40 and Cove Road.

25 General Robert E. Lee

With Longstreet's Corp entered Hagerstown September 11, 1862 to make it a base for operations in Pennsylvania. On September 14, 1862 this force hastened to the battle of South Mountain and then to the Battlefield of Antietam.   (1)

Alt. U.S. 40, south of Wilson Boulevard.

26 An Indian Deed

Israel Friend in 1727 secured a deed from the Indian Chiefs of the Five Nations. Beginning "at the mouth of Andietum Creek thence up the Potomack River 200 shoots as fur as an arrow can be slung out of a bow" thence "100 shoots right back from the river" then "squared till it intercedes with the creek". (1)

Harpers Ferry Road and Limekiln Road, south end of bridge over creek.

 John Brown

And his associates collected arms and ammunition on the Kennedy Farm (Samples Manor) in Maryland for months prior to the raid on the arsenal at Harpers

Ferry, October 17, 1859.   (1)

Chestnut Grove and Harper's Ferry Roads MD 73 at Harpers Ferry Bridge.

28 Jonathan Hager House

circa 1740

October 16, 1739, Johnathan Hager took up "Hager's Fancy" 200 acres in the valley of Antietam Creek. A year later he married Elizabeth Kershner for whom Elizabeth-Town (Hagerstown) was named and established his home here. In 1944 it was acquired by the Washington County Historical Society.   (1)

Virginia Avenue at Key Street, Hagerstown.

29 Jones' Crossroads

This crossing served during July 10-15, 1863, as an anchor for the flanks of such gathering Federal Forces as the Reserve Artillery and the Second, Third and Twelfth Corps. Minor skirmishes with elements of Lee's besieged Army of Northern Virginia occurred here.   (48)

MD 68 just east of MD 65.

30 Keller Home

used to treat Confederate Officer

During Battle of Funkstown July 10, 1863, Major H. D. McDaniel, 110th Georgia Regiment, suffered a severe wound and brought to this home. He survived to later become Governor of Georgia.   (4)

U.S. 40A in Funkstown.

31 Kennedy Farm

This farmhouse was used as the staging area for John Brown and his small army for their historic raid on Harpers Ferry, Virginia - October 10, 1859 - an act which so aroused public outrage, north and south, that it ignited the great American Civil War. It can be said… "It all started here."   (46)

Chestnut Grove Road.

32 Lancelot Jacques

A French Huguenot who in partnership with Thomas Johnson in 1768 built "Greenspring Furnace." He and Johnson dissolved partnership in 1776 when Johnson became the first Governor of Maryland. Jacques' house built about 1766.   (1)

MD 56, west of McCoy Ferry Road.

Washington Monument

Fort Frederick

㉝   **The Long Meadow**

Originally patented 1739 to Colonel Thomas Cresap. Acquired 1746 by Daniel Dulany. Sold 1763 to Colonel Henry Bouquet. Let by his will to Colonel Haldimand. Acquired 1773 by General Joseph Springs. Purchased 1789 by Thomas Hart, partner of Nathaniel Rochester (founder of Rochester, New York). Hart's daughter born here, married Henry Clay. Bought in 1827 by the United States at public sale. (1)

Marsh Pike, 1.2 miles north of Lonemeadow Road, north of Hagerstown.

㉞   **Mason-Dixon Line**
100th Mile Stone

Maryland-Pennsylvania boundary line. Surveyed and marked 1763-68 by two English astronomers, Charles Mason and Jeremiah Dixon. This is one of the "Crown" Stones, set every five miles displaying the Coat of Arms of Lord Baltimore on south and the Penns on north sides. Intermediate miles marked by Stones with M facing Maryland and P - Pennsylvania. Stones imported from England. (1)

On Marsh Pike, opposite 100th Mile Stone.

㉟   **Mason-Dixon Line**
105th Mile Stone

500 feet beyond this point, in the garden of the first house, this stone is located. It bears the Coat of Arms of Lord Baltimore and William Penn. The 104th Mile Stone and 103rd Mile Stone bear the letters M and P, Maryland-Pennsylvania and are located along the Maryland edge of this road. (1)

Marsh Pile, south of Pennsylvania Line.

㊱   **McCoy's Ferry**

On May 23, 1861, Confederates attempting to capture the Ferry Boat at McCoy's Landing were driven off by the Clear Spring Guard. Here on October 10, 1862, General J.E.B. Stuart crossed the Potomac on his second ride around McClellan's Army. (7)

C & O Canal at McCoy's Ferry near McCoy's Ferry Road.

WASHINGTON MONUMENT - Volunteers from Bonsboro celebrated Independence day, July 4, 1827, by erecting the first monument to honor George Washington in the country. (See page 119, marker 47). **FORT FREDERICK** - Located in the western part of the county, Fort Frederick was built in 1756 to protect Maryland from the French and the Indians. (See page 117, marker 20).

37 **"Old Mr. Flint's" Home**

George Washington's diary (while he visited Berkley Springs in 1769) states: "August 30 Old Mr. Flint dined with us" and on September 4: "Rid to the Potomac where my hourses were. From thence to Mr. Flint's and to the Pennsylvania Line, and returned to dinner." (1)

MD 144, 1.5 miles west of Hancock.

38 **Old Slave Block**

From 1800 to 1865 this stone was used as a slave auction block. It has been a famous landmark at this original location for over 150 years. (1)

Southwest corner of MD 65 and MD 34 in Sharpsburg.

39 **One of Lee's Ammunition Trains**

Was captured here September 15, 1862 by 1200 Federal Cavalry under Colonel B. F. Davis, escaping from General T. I. "Stonewall" Jackson's capture of Harpers Ferry. This loss was felt by the Confederate Army at the Battle of Antietam. (1)

U.S. 11, between Hagerstown and Williamsport.

40 **Rose Hill**

Part of an original grant of 10,000 acres known as Conococheague Manor. The mansion house was built early in the 1800's and tradition attributes its design to Benjamin H. Latrobe. It is noted for its Adam Woodwork and for its great wall with a hanging staircase. (4)

MD 63, 0.5 mile south east of MD 68.

41 **Springfield Farm**
(circa 1755)

Home of Brigadier General Otho Holland Williams, Revolutionary War Hero and Founder, 1786, of Williamsport; and of Colonel Elie Williams, President of Commission to lay out National Road and Chief Surveyour Chesapeake and Ohio Canal. President George Washington dined here October 20, 1790, while considering Williamsport as possible site of Federal Capital. (4)

U.S. 11, northeast of MD 63 Springfield Lane.

42 **Stonewall Jackson's Way**

Under special order 191, Major General Thomas J. Jackson led Confederate Troops from Frederick to capture Harper's Ferry. On September 11, 1862, Jackson's Second Corps moved by this road from its encampment near Boonsborough to cross the Potomac at Williamsport. (7)

MD 68 and Lappans Road.

43 **Saint Thomas Church**
founded 1835

During 1861-62 the church was used as a hospital by Union Troops of 39th Illinois Regular Volunteers, 5th Connecticut Regular Volunteers, 46th Pennsylvania Regular Volunteers, 28th New York Regular Volunteers. Under Colonel Williams their Batteries were placed around and behind the church to repel Stonewall Jackson's Batteries, on the opposite hill in West Virginia. (1)

MD 144 and Church Street, Hancock.

44 **Saint Thomas' Episcopal Parish**

Saint Thomas' Episcopal Parish founded 1835 used as a Union Hospital 1862-63. (47)

High Street and Church Road at Church, Hagerstown.

45 **Tonoloway Fort**

Lieutenant Stoddert and twenty men erected and garrisoned a block house and stockaded fort near here on the property of Evan Shelby in 1755 after Braddock's defeat. It was abandoned in 1756-57 after Fort Frederick was completed. (1)

Western edge of Hancock.

46 **Washington County**

The first county in the United States named for the Father of his Country. Erected out of Frederick County 1776. It then included what is now Alleghany and Garrett Counties.

Other Side
Frederick County

Named for Frederick the 5th and last Lord Baltimore. Erected out of Prince George's County in 1748. It then included Montgomery County and all of Maryland west to the West Virginia boundary. (1)

U.S. 340 at County Line.

47 **Washington Monument**

Volunteer villagers of nearby Boonsboro celebrated their Independence Day, July 4, 1827, by building and dedicating this first monument to the memory of George Washington. Repaired and altered many times over a hundred years by patriotic citizens, it was finally restored to its original design in 1934-36 by the Civilian Conservation Corps (CCC). This monument, used by the Union Army during the Civil War as a signal station, and it's surrounding land was bought by the Washington County Historical Society in 1922 and presented to the State of Maryland for park development in 1934. This massive structure was certified a "Maryland Historical Monument" in March, 1972 and a "National Historical Monument" in November 1972. (50)

Washington Monument State Park, near Boonsboro.

48 **Williamsport**

Williamsport was used by Union General Patterson crossing on July 2, 1861, Confederate General Jackson moving against Harper's Ferry on September 11, 1862, and General Lee advancing with much of his army to, and retreating from, Gettysburg in June and July, 1863. (7)

U.S. 11, northeast of MD 63.

49 **Williamsport**
(Conococheague)

An important point during the French and Indian War 1753-1758. George Washington given authority to locate the "Federal City" at any point on the Potomac between Conococheague and the Eastern Branch. He inspected this site October 1790 but chose the present District of Columbia. (1)

U.S. 11, northeast of MD 63 .

50 **Wilson Bridge**
(Link between East and West)

Built in 1819, this five-arch structure, named for nearby village, was first stone bridge in Washington County. Erected by Silas Harry at cost of $12,000. It was a major improvement to road system between Baltimore and Cumberland, providing continuous smooth surface from Eastern Seaboard to Western Wilderness. It is one of two oldest bridges remaining on the National Pike (first federally financed road in the U.S.). Wilson Bridge carried traffic until seriously damaged by storm flooding in 1972. (45)

East side of Conococheague Creek on Old U.S. 40.

Cumberland

Western Maryland Scenic Railroad

Toll Gate House

TOLL GATE HOUSE - in LaVale was erected in 1833 after the completion of this section of the original National Road. (See page 121, marker 5). **CUMBERLAND** - Nestled in a large valley this historic city was once a boom town. The B&O Railroad, the C&O Canal, and the National Road all converged here. **WESTERN MARYLAND SCENIC RAILROAD** - With the decline of rail transportation in the 1950's and 60's much of the rail lines going to Cumberland decreased operation. The Western Maryland Scenic Railroad attracts thousands for a ride on their steam engine powered trains from Cumberland to Frostburg.

ALLEGANY COUNTY

1 Billmeyer Game Refuge

165 acres, purchased December 15th, 1923 from Frank Billmeyer, from Hunter's License fund, for the purpose of propagating game. (3)

Old U.S. 40 between Hancock and Cumberland.

2 "Braddock's Road"

Near this point, on June 10, 1755, after nearly a month's delay at Fort Cumberland, Braddock's Troops started towards Fort Duquesne to wrest it from the French. On July 9, 1755 he met his terrible defeat at the Monongahela. (1)

U.S. 220 (Green Road) and MD 49 (Braddock Road).

3 Clarysville Hospital

Clarysville Inn, built in 1807, was the main building of the Clarysville Army Hospital during the Civil War. Temporary barracks nearby housed hundreds of wounded and sick Union Soldiers. After 1862 the overflow of patients received medical care in Cumberland. (7)

Alt. U.S. 40, Plaque mounted on Clarysville Inn.

4 The First Iron Rails

Made in the United States were manufactured in 1844 at Mount Savage. Before that time all iron rails were imported from England. (1)

Alt. U.S. 40 near Mt. Savage Road.

5 First Toll Gate House

On the Old National (Cumberland) Road. Erected about 1833 after this portion of the road was turned over to the State of Maryland by the United States Government. There was one other Toll Gate in Maryland on this road. (1)

U.S. 40 west of MD 53.

6 Folck's Mill

Here in Evitts Creek Valley on August 1, 1864, General McCausland's Confederate Cavalry, returning after burning Chambersburg, was surprised by General Kelley's Union Troops from Cumberland. The Confederates were repulsed and retreated across the Potomac at Old Town. (7)

East of Cumberland on U.S. 40 near the Shrine County Club.

7 Jane Frazier

Wife of Lieutenant John Frazier was captured by the Indians near this spot in October 1755 and taken to the Miami River. She escaped after eighteen months and made her way back to her home.

MD 51, 0.5 miles south of Evitts Creek.

8 "Martin's Plantation"

General Braddock's 2nd Camp on the march to Fort Duquesne, June 14th, 15th, 1755. The Old Braddock Road passed to the south-east of the National Road from Clarysville to the "Shades of Death" near "Two Mile Run". The National Road was begun by the government in 1811. (1)

U.S. 40, east Main Street, Frostburg.

9 In Memory of
Col. Thomas Cresap
Pathfinder - Pioneer - Patriot

Built the first home and fort in this county at Oldtown, about 1740. Surveyed the first trail to the west, starting near this spot in 1751. His sons - Daniel Cresap, for whom Dan's Mountain is named; Thomas Cresap, Jr. killed in battle with the Indians on Savage Mountain; Michael Cresap, Captain in Dunmore's War, First Captain Rifle Battalions, Revolutionary War, whose grave is in Trinity Church Yard, New York City. His grandsons - Sons of Daniel Cresap - Capt. Michael Cresap, Jr., Lieutenant Daniel Cresap, Jr., Lieutenant Joseph Cresap of Dunmore's and Revolutionary Wars. (9)

Monument with plaque in Riverside Park, Cumberland.

10 Michael Cresap

He built his house, which can be seen nearby, about 1764. A trader, he cleared wilderness and fought Indians in "Cresap's War" in Ohio, 1774. As a Captain he led riflemen, some painted Indian-style, to Boston at the start of the Revolution. Because of failing health he attempted to return home but died on the way and is buried in Trinity Churchyard, New York City. A brick addition to the house was built about 1781. (5)

MD 51 near western entrance to Old Town.

11 Military Hospital

On this site stood Belvedere Hall. During the Civil War this hall was used as a military hospital. (7)

Plaque on front of First Federal Savings and Loan Building, Baltimore Street, Cumberland.

12 Military Hospital

On this site stood the First Presbyterian Church. During the Civil War it was used as a military hospital. (7)

Plaque on north side of building at 16 North Liberty Street, Cumberland.

13 Mount Savage Iron Works
1839

In 1844. the first iron rails made in the United States were produced on this spot by the Mount Savage Iron Works. Erected in 1839, the iron works contributed extensively to the development of the Mount Savage Community. (4)

MD 36 and Calla Hill Road.

14 "The Narrows"

One of the most picturesque spots around Cumberland. Discovered by Spendelow after the road over Wills Mountain had been constructed by General Braddock. Adopted as the route of the Cumberland Road (The National Road) 1833. The old stone bridge across Wills Creek was used from 1834 to 1932. (1)

At the Narrows Bridge on Alt. U.S. 40, west of Cumberland.

15 The National Road
(Called the Cumberland Road)

Was the first of the internal improvements

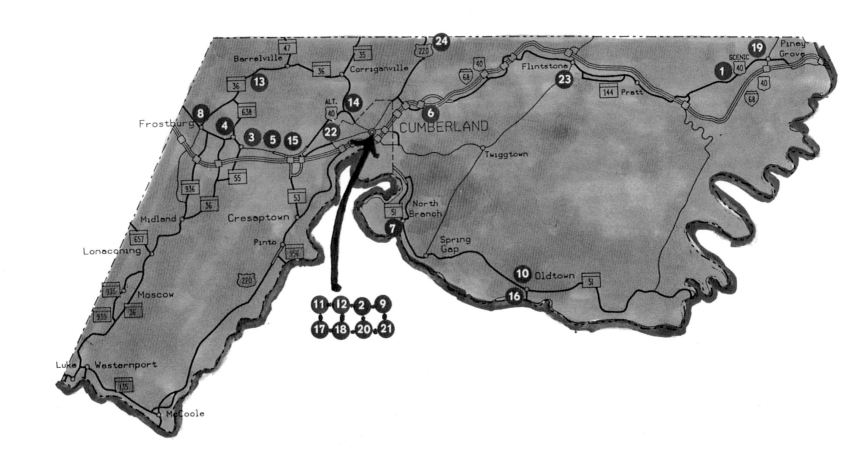

ALLEGANY COUNTY

Allegany County lies just west of Washington County and was named after an Indian word which means "beautiful stream". Allegany County became a transportation center early in its history. In Cumberland the C&O Canal, the B&O Railroad and the National Road all met and the town became an early gateway to the Ohio Valley and the land further west.

undertaken by the U.S. Government. Surveys were authorized in 1806 over the route of "Braddock's Road", which followed "Nemacolin's Path", an Indian trail, over which George Washington traveled in 1754 to Fort LeBoeuf. (1)

Alt. U.S. 40, 3 miles west of Cumberland.

Old Town
(King Opessa's Town)

Fording place for "Great Warriors Path" of the "Five Nations" from New York to the south. Thomas Cresap built stockade fort here in 1741, used as refuge during French and Indian War after Braddock's Defeat. George Washington was here on his first visit to Maryland 1748 and often thereafter. (1)

MD 51 near western entrance to Old Town.

On This Site Originally Stood The

Headquarters of George Washington. Since removed to Riverside Park. He was entertained at David Lynn's House (which later occupied this site) when he came here in 1794 to review the troops during the Whiskey Rebellion. (1)

Washington Street and Prospect Square, Cumberland

The Parade Ground of Fort Cumberland

Occupied this site 1755. Here the Indians envoys were received before Braddock left for his defeat. In 1756-58 the garrison under Col. Washington was still reviewed here. (1)

Washington Street and Prospect Square at Court House.

⑲ Perry Barnes Game Refuge

50 Acres, purchased December 13, 1930, from Perry Barnes and wife, from Hunter's License Fund for the purpose of propagating game. (3)

Old U.S. 40 between Hancock and Cumberland.

⑳ The Site of Old Fort Cumberland

This Tablet marks the site of Old Fort Cumberland which was built in 1755 by order of the British Government and named in honor of The Duke of Cumberland, Captain General of the British Army. It was the base of military operations of General Edward Braddock and Colonel George Washington in the French and Indian War (8)

On the wall of Emmanual Church, Washington Street, Cumberland.

㉑ Site of Fort Cumberland

The store houses of the Ohio Company were first located near this point. In 1754 the first fort (called Mt. Pleasant) was built. General Edward Braddock enlarged the fort in 1755 and renamed it after his friend the Duke of Cumberland. (1)

Episcopal Church Yard, U.S. 220 (Green Street) and Washington Street.

㉒ "Spendelow Camp"
Also called "Camp at the Grove"

General Braddock's 1st Camp on the march from Fort Cumberland to Fort Duquesne, June 11th to 13th 1755. After building a road over Wills Mountain, Spendelow, an engineer, discovered a route by "The Narrows" and Braddock's Run and a second road was opened. (1)

MD 49 and Vocke Road.

㉓ "The Warrior's Path"

War path of the five nations from central New York to the mountains of the Carolinas. One of the longest Indian Trails in America, crossed this highway about this point. (1)

Alt. U.S. 40 in front of Flintstone High School.

㉔ Washington's Road

By order of Colonel Bouquet, George Washington's Troops opened this road from Fort Cumberland to Reastown (Bedford PA) during July 1758. Bouquet and Washington conferred half way between these places July 30, 1758. (1)

U.S. 220, just south of the Maryland - Pennsylvania State Line.

Muddy Creek Falls

Deep Creek Lake

Valley North of McHenry

MUDDY CREEK FALLS - The natural beauty of Garrett County is as stunning as it was in the early 19th century when Henry Ford, Thomas A. Edison and Harvey Firestone camped here. (See page 125, marker 3). **DEEP CREEK LAKE** - This is the largest lake in Maryland, it is renowned for its fishing, canoeing and boating. **SCENIC VALLEY** - This valley is close to the site of Meshack Brownings' grave, it reflects the area which made Browning Maryland's most famous hunter. (See page 125, marker 14).

GARRETT COUNTY

❶ Bear Camp

General Braddock's 6th Camp on the march to Fort Duquesne Saturday and Sunday, June 20th and 21st, 1755. Washington was forced to remain behind with a guard on account of "violent fevers" until cured by "Dr. James Powders (one of the most excellent medicines in the world)", he wrote his brother Augustine.   (1)

U.S. 40, 0.3 miles south of the Pennsylvania line at Oakton.

❷ Bear Creek Trout Hatchery and Rearing Station

Garrett County

One and one-half miles from this point. Purchased by state 1928.   (2)

U.S. 219 and road leading to Bear Creek.

❸ Campsite

In August 1918 and again in July 1921, Henry Ford, Thomas A. Edison, Harvey Firestone, John Burroughs and company encamped here by Muddy Creek Falls.   (4)

Muddy Creek Falls in Swallows Falls State Park

❹ Casselman River Bridge

When built in 1813, this structure was the longest single-span stonebridge in America. The high arch was designed to facilitate riverboat traffic on the proposed C&O Canal. However, due to the emerging railroad industry in the nineteenth century, the C&O Canal was never extended beyond Cumberland, MD. Restored in 1911 the Casselman Bride is now listed on the National Register of Historic Sites. It has become a world renowned tourist attraction, a delight to photographers, artists and historians and is often prominent in photographic and art exhibits. This bridge is the oldest of three bridges which span the Casselman River at Little Crossings. The three bridges tell the region's story of transportation, settlement and development.   (6)

At east abutment of bridge located near Penn Alps.

❺ Castleman's River Bridge

(formerly "Little Youghiogheny")

Erected in 1813 by David Shriver, Jr., Superintendent of the "Cumberland Road"

(The National Road). This 80 foot span was the largest stone arch in America at the time. It was continuously used from 1813 to 1933.   (1)

U.S. 40, 0.2 miles east of Grantsville.

❻ Charles Friend's Home

George Washington stopped here September 26, 1784 on his trip to determine a feasible passage between the Potomac and the Ohio for a canal or easy portage between these rivers as a passage to the western territory.   (1)

MD 39, 2.5 miles east of Oakland.

❼ Cleveland Cottage and Site of Deer Park Hotel

The hotel was built by the Baltimore and Ohio Railroad. Opened July 4, 1873, and operated until 1929. Dismantled 1942. President and Mrs. Grover Cleveland spent their honeymoon at the Cottage in June 1886.   (4)

MD 135, 0.5 miles west of Sand Flat Road, Deer Park.

❽ Cleveland Cottages

President Grover Cleveland and his bride, the former Frances Folson, arrived here the day following their White House Wedding on June 2, 1886. They spent their honeymoon at this Deer Park Hotel Cottage.   (4)

On Hotel Road, 0.5 miles south of Main Street in Deer Park.

❾ Colonel James McHenry Of Baltimore (1753-1816)

Aide to Gen. George Washington during the Revolution, McHenry was a physician, signer of the Constitution from Maryland and Secretary of War from 1796 to 1800. Named in his honor was the Baltimore Fort that withstood the British bombardment Sept. 13-14, 1814. He purchased, circa 1805, land near here in what was then called Buffalo Marsh and Cherry Tree Meadows, and this settlement took his name.   (5)

U.S. 219 Scenic Overlook, Deep Creek Lake.

❿ Deep Creek Lake Garrett County

Property of the Youghiogheny Hydro Electric Corporation of the Associated Gas and Electric System. Lake under the supervision of the Conservation Department of Maryland. The following streams flow into

the lake: Deep and Cherry Creeks, North and Green Glades, Meadow Mountain, Piney, Poland, Pawn, Gravley, Marsh, Smith and Bull's Arm Runs.   (2)

U.S. 219 at Information Center.

⓫ Deer Park Hotel

Built by the B&O Railroad, opened July 4, 1873 and operated until 1929. Razed 1942. This was one of the most exclusive mountain resorts in the East. Many nationally prominent people, including four United States Presidents, were guests here.   (4)

Hotel Drive and Haines Road in Deer Park.

⓬ Friend's Graveyard

Nearby are the graves of John Friend, Sr. (1732-1808). Kerrenhappuch Hyatt (D. 1798), his wife, and their son Gabriel (1761-1852). John and Gabriel were soldiers in the Revolution. The first permanent settlers in Garrett County. They settled on the Youghiogheny River at"Friend's Fortune", now known as Friendsville.   (4)

MD 42, 0.2 miles west of Youghiogheny River Bridge.

⓭ General Braddlock's 5th Camp

On the march to Fort Duquesne June 19th, 1755. By Washington's advice, Braddock pushed forward from Little Meadows to this camp with 1200 chosen men and officers leaving the heavy artillery and baggage behind to follow by easy stages under Colonel Dunbar.   (1)

U.S. 40, 25 feet east of bridge over Big Shade Run, west of Grantsville.

⓮ The Grave of Meshack Browning

(1781 - 1859)

Born at Damascus, Maryland, Garrett County's most famous hunter. Browning wrote the book, "Forty-Four Years of the Life of a Hunter". During this time he killed two thousand deer and five hundred bear.   (4)

MD 42, 0.3 miles south of HoyesSang Run Road.

⓯ Hoye-Crest

Highest point in Maryland, Backbone Mountain, Garrett County. 3360 feet above sea level. Named for Captain Charles E.

GARRETT COUNTY

The western most county of the state, Garrett County is also the highest, the newest, and has the largest lake in the state. One fifth of the county consists of public parks, lakes, and recreation areas.

Hoye, founder of the Garrett County Historical Society. Dedicated September 1, 1952.　　(4)

U.S. 219 at West Virginia Line.

16　"The Little Crossings"

(Of the Little Youghiogheny River, now called Castleman's River)

So called by George Washington when he crossed on June 19, 1755, with General Edward Braddock on the ill fated expedition to Fort Duquesne (Pittsburgh).　　(1)

U.S. 40, at Castleman's River Bridge, 0.3 miles east of Granstville.

17　Little Meadows

General Braddock's 4th Camp on the march to Fort Duquesne June 17th, 1755. Washington arrived here after Braddock's defeat July 15th, 1755. Washington also stopped here May 9th, 1754, July 7th or 8th, 1754, October 1st, 1770, November 26th, 1770, and September 10th 1784.　　(1)

U.S. 40, at Piney Run Creek, 3 miles east of Grantsville.

18　"McCulloch's Path"

(Named for an Early Pioneer)

The first trail through the Glades passed near this point. George Washington, on his visit here in September 1784, wrote of it: "McCulloch's Path which owes its origin to buffaloes, being no other than their tracks from one lick to another". "Archy's Spring" is nearby.　　(1)

U.S. 219, 3.5 miles south of Oakland.

19　"Savage River Camp"

General Braddock's 3rd Camp on his March to Fort Duquesne June 16, 1755. The Route, later known as the Old Braddock Road, passed to the southeast of the National Road. Captain Orme's diary says "We entirely demolished three wagons and shattered several" descending Savage Mountain.　　(1)

U.S. 40, 1.5 miles west of the Alleghany County Line.

20　Thayer Game Refuge

1029 acres, purchased June 28, 1927, from John O. Thayer, from Hunter's License fund, for the purpose of propagating game.　　(3)

U.S. 219, 11 miles north of Oakland.

SWALLOW FALLS - Swallow Falls State Park reflects the beauty which has attracted visitors to this area for years. This whole area is perfect for hiking, fishing, horse back riding and just enjoying the scenery. (See page 125, marker 3).

QUESTIONS

To assist you with your appreciation of the information on these historic roadside markers I have put together a series of questions. This is a "win-win" quiz because we have given you the location of each answer. We hope you will find the answers both interesting and informative.

1. Where were the first iron rails made in the United States?
   (Answer: See Allegany County)

2. Who built and owned Greenbelt?
   (Answer: See Prince George's County)

3. Who directed all Confederate military prisons east of the Mississippi?
   (Answer: See Wicomico County)

4. Under what town marker is George Washington's grandmother mentioned?
   (Answer: See Wicomico County)

5. What is the name of the first road built by colonists in Maryland?
   (Answer: See St. Mary's County)

6. Where was the Capital of Maryland from 1634 to 1694?
   (Answer: See St. Mary's County)

7. How were early colonial road markers made?
   (Answer: See St. Mary's County)

8. Where did the colonists land in Maryland in 1634?
   (Answer: See St. Mary's County)

9. Who was the last survivor of the signers of the Declaration of Independence?
   (Answer: See Howard County)

10. Over what river was the first iron rail road bridge built in America?
    (Answer: See Howard County)

11. Who made the bronze doors to the Capitol in Washington?
    (Answer: See Carroll County)

12. Who was the first preacher of the Methodists in America?
    (Answer: See Carroll County)

13. The first trail through the glades owes its origin to what?
    (Answer: See Garrett County)

14. What is the highest point in Maryland?
    (Answer: See Garrett County)

15. For whom was Fort McHenry named?
    (Answer: See Garrett County)

16. What was Askiminokonson?
    (Answer: See Worcester County)

17. Who commanded the sloop of war "Reprisal" that took Benjamin Franklin to France in 1776?
    (Answer: See Kent County)

18. In 1789 where did George Washington receive his Doctor of Laws degree?
    (Answer: See Kent County)

19. What is the oldest building in the country used continuously for medical education?
    (Answer: See Baltimore City)

20. What is the first Dental College in the world?
    (Answer: See Baltimore City)

21. Where is Francis Scott Key's original manuscript of "The Star-Spangled Banner"?
    (Answer: See Baltimore City)

22. Where was the "U.S. Frigate Constellation", now in the Inner Harbor, launched?
    (Answer: See Baltimore City)

23. What current Maryland city was originally part of the Choptank Indian Reservation.
    (Answer: See Dorchester County)

24. Who was known as the "Moses of her People," as well as served the Union Army as a nurse, scout, and spy?
    (Answer: See Dorchester County)

25. What was Chicacone?
    (Answer: See Dorchester County)

26. Where is the oldest courthouse in continuous use in Maryland?
    (Answer: See Queen Anne's County)

27. Name the Chief Justice of the United States who administered the Presidential Oath to Van Buren, Harrison, Polk, Taylor, Pierce, Buchanan, and Lincoln?
    (Answer: See Calvert County)

28. Who was the Maryland astronomer who was a colleague of Sir Isaac Newton, and whose data was quoted repeatedly in Newton's scientific works?
    (Answer: See Calvert County)

29. Who was the first elected Governor of Maryland in 1777?
    (Answer: See Calvert County)

30. What was " The Bush Declaration" ?
    (Answer: See Harford County)

31. Where was the first Methodist College in the world established?
    (Answer: See Harford County)

32. Who was the first graduate of medicine in America?
    (Answer: See Harford County)

33. In London, in 1850, what slate was judged best in the world?
(Answer: See Harford County)

34. Where was William Paca, signer of The Declaration of Independence, born?
(Answer: See Harford County)

35. From where did the stones used to mark the Mason-Dixon Line originate?
(Answer: See Harford County)

36. Where is General George Washington's grandmother buried?
(Answer: See Somerset County)

37. Where did President Madison and his family take refuge when the British burned the Capitol and the White House?
(Answer: See Montgomery County)

38. Where was President Lincoln when he came under Confederate fire?
(Answer: See Montgomery County)

39. Who was General Washington's Aide-de-Camp from 1776-1783?
(Answer: See Talbot County)

40. Who was the first Superintendent of the Naval Academy, who later became Senior Officer in the Confederate Navy?
(Answer: See Talbot County)

41. Who was the first native of the United States to be canonized a saint?
(Answer: See Frederick County)

42. When was Annapolis the Capital of the United States?
(Answer: See Anne Arundel County)

43. Approximately how many Confederate and Union Soldiers were at the Battle of Antietam?
(Answer: See Washington County)

44. Who founded the City of Rochester, New York?
(Answer: See Washington County)

45. The Mason-Dixon Line was named for whom?
(Answer: See Washington County)

46. Who was the president of the commission to lay out the National Road and the Chief Surveyor of the Chesapeake and Ohio Canal?
(Answer: See Washington County)

47. Name a town, other than Washington D.C., that was considered as a site for our nations capital?
(Answer: See Washington County)

48. When was the first monument to George Washington dedicated?
(Answer: See Washington County)

49. Where was the first military airfield in the United States?
(Answer: See Prince George's County)

50. Where was the first experimental farm and first agricultural college in the Western Hemisphere?
(Answer: See Prince George's County)

51. Who authored the Philippines first Constitution?
(Answer: See Caroline County)

52. In 1863, where were the 7th, 9th, 19th, and 30th United States Infantry recruited and trained?
(Answer: See Charles County)

53. What famous doctor was tried and imprisoned on Dry Tortugas Island?
(Answer: See Charles County)

54. Who commanded the noted Confederate raider the "Alabama"?
(Answer: See Charles County)

55. In 1670, what did Governor Charles Calvert present to the King of the Mattawoman Indians as a gift?
(Answer: See Charles County)

56. To whom did Detective Captain William Williams unsuccessfully offer $100,000 reward for information that would lead to the capture of John Wilkes Booth?
(Answer: See Charles County)

57. Who was the self-educated mathematician and astronomer who assisted in surveying the District of Columbia?
(Answer: See Baltimore County)

58. What was called the "Bulldog at Baltimore Gate"?
(Answer: See Baltimore County)

59. What was the point closest to Baltimore reached by the Confederate Troops during the Civil War?
(Answer: See Baltimore County)

60. Where was chrome first discovered in the United States?
(Answer: See Baltimore County)

61. Who commanded the sloop "Wasp" during the War of 1812?
(Answer: See Cecil County)

62. Who wrote "Robinson Crusoe" ?
(Answer: See Cecil County)

63. Augustine Washington (father of George) owned one-twelfth in what Maryland company?
(Answer: See Cecil County)

64. Captain John Smith first named what Maryland river the Tochwough River?
(Answer: See Cecil County)

SPONSORS

1. State Road Commission
2. Conservation Department of Maryland, Swepson Earle, Commissioner
3. E. Lee Le'Compte, State Game Warden of Maryland
4. Maryland Historical Society
5. Maryland Bicentennial Commission and Maryland Historical Society
6. Spruce Forrest Artisan History Walk
7. Maryland Civil War Centennial Commission
8. Cresap Chapter, Daughters of the American Revolution
9. Cresap Society
10. Caroline County Historical Society
11. Tourism Council - Upper Chesapeake, Denton Jaycees, Caroline County Historical Society and Maryland Historical Society
12. Society of Colonial Wars and Maryland Historical Society
13. Choptank Bicentennial Committee
14. Maryland Department of Transportation and Maryland Historical Society
15. The Newton Association, Inc. and Maryland Historical Society
16. Wicomico County Historical Society and Maryland Historical Society
17. Maryland Historic Trust
18. Col. Thomas Dorsey Chapter, Daughters of the American Revolution
19. Carter Braxton Chapter, Daughters of the American Revolution
20. International Right of War Association, Potomac Chapter No. 14 and Maryland Historical Society
21. Friends of Trinity and Maryland Historical Society
22. Historical Society of Harford County
23. Governor William Paca Chapter, Daughters of the American Revolution
24. John Eager Howard Chapter, Daughters of the American Revolution
25. Bicentennial Committee of Aberdeen and Maryland Historical Society
26. Bel Air Rotary Club and Historical Society of Harford County
27. Garden Club of Harford County
28. Citizens of Harford County and Maryland Historical Society

29. The Captain Jeremiah Baker Chapter, Daughters of the American Revolution of Cecil County
30. State of Maryland
31. George Washington Bi-Centennial Daughters of the American Revolution Marker, Dorset Chapter N.S.D.A.R.
32. Historical Society of Cecil County
33. Colonial Charlestown, Incorporated and Maryland Historical Society
34. Historical Society of Cecil County, Woman's Club of Elkton, Assoc., Cecil Endeavors, Inc., and Maryland Historical Society
35. Port Deposit Heritage, Inc., and Maryland Historical Society
36. Perryville Bicentennial Committee and Maryland Historical Society
37. Elk Neck Bicentennial Committee and Maryland Historical Society
38. Bald Friar Bicentennial Community
39. Calvert Heritage Association and Maryland Historical Society
40. Colonel Henry Hollingsworth Chapter, Sons of the American Revolution and Maryland Historical Society
41. Scott's United Methodist Church, Trappe Bicentennial Committee and Talbot County Bicentennial Committee
42. St. Michaels Bicentennial Commission and Maryland Historical Society
43. Talbot County Council, Society of Cincinnati of Maryland, Historical Society of Talbot County, Inc., and Maryland Historical Society
44. Vestry of Old Wye Episcopal Church and Maryland Historical Society
45. Maryland Historical Society and Washington Committee, Maryland Historical Society
46. National Historical Landmark
47. Washington County Historical Society
48. Maryland Civil War Heritage Commission
49. Women of the Moose, Hagerstown Chapter
50. Department of Natural Resources
51. Erected by United States
52. The National Society of Descendants of Lords of the Maryland Manors and the Maryland Historical Society
53. State Roads Commission and St. Mary's County Historical Society

54. St. Mary's County Historical Society and Maryland Historical Society
55. County Commissioner's of Queen Anne's County
56. Ladies of St. Peter's Alter and Rosary Society
57. Queen Anne's County Bicentennial Commission and Maryland Historical Society
58. Queen Anne's County Garden Club
59. Bennett's Point Improvement Association and Maryland Historical Society
60. Queen Anne's County Historical Society and Maryland Historical Society
61. George Washington Bicentennial Committee of Frederick County
62. Mount Olivet Cemetery Board of Managers
63. Frederick Chapter, N.S.D.A.R.
64. The Kiwanis Club of Frederick
65. Frederick Chapter Daughters of the American Revolution
66. Federation of Rural Women's Clubs of Frederick County
67. Seton Shrine Center and Maryland Historical Society
68. William J. Grove, Lime Kiln, MD
69. St. Joseph's College Alumnae Association and Maryland Historical Society
70. Methodist Historical Society
71. Carroll County Civil War Centennial Commission
72. Mrs. Paul J. Nowland through the Delaware Civil War Centennial Commission
73. The Patriotic Order Sons of America
74. Board of Calvert County Commissioners, Calvert County Historical Society, and Maryland Historical Society
75. Calvert County Historical Society and Maryland Historical Society
76. East New Market Heritage Foundation and Maryland Historical Society
77. East New Market Town Council and Maryland Historical Society
78. Rock Community Improvement League
79. Dorchester Historical Society
80. Dorchester County Historical Society
81. Loch Raven Improvement Association and Board of Trustees of Taylor Chapter, St. John's of Hamilton United Methodist Church
82. Roland Park Garden Club, Roland Park Civic

League, and Maryland Historical Society

John Hopkins Alumni of Alpha Delta Phi

Society of Colonial Wars in the State of Maryland

The Alumni Association

Maryland State Society Daughter of the American Colonists

Canton Improvement Association

Church Home and Hospital and Maryland Historical Society

London Bridge Chapter Daughters of the American Revolution

Society for the Preservation of Maryland Antiquities

Old Kent Chapter Daughters of the American Revolution

The Men's Club of Chester Parish

The Citizens of Rock Hall

Kent Lodge 74 Instituted 1851, Massey Lodge 157 Instituted 1914, Independent Order of Odd Fellows

"Friends of Martin Wagner", the Historical Society of Kent County and the Maryland Historical Society

The Citizens of Chestertown

Anonymous Marylanders

Captain Lambert Wicks Foundation and Maryland Historical Society

Kent County Commissioners Miller, Rasin, and Harris and the Maryland Historical Society

100. Baltimore County Historical Society

101. Colonel Nicholas Ruxton Moore Chapter, Sons of the American Revolution

102. Rotary Club of Dundalk, Inc., Innerwheel of Dundalk and Maryland Historical Society

103. Patapsco Neck Bicentennial Committee and Maryland Historical Society

104. The Sudbrook Club and Maryland Historical Society

105. Baltimore County Historical Society and Maryland Historical Society

106. Dundalk-Patapsco Neck Historical Society

107. Maryland Division, United Daughters of the Confederacy, Baltimore County Historical Society and Maryland Historical Society

108. Centennial Committee Glyndan Community Association

109. The Friends of St. John's Chapel, Baltimore County Historical Trust, and Maryland Historical Society

110. Rockland Homeowners Association and Maryland Historical Society

111. The Montgomery County Historical Society and the Maryland House and Garden Pilgrimage

112. United Daughters of the Confederacy, Maryland Division

113. Maryland Historical Society and Damascus Bicentennial Commission

114. Maryland-National Capital Park and Planning Commission and Montgomery County Park Commission

115. Montgomery County Historical Society

116. Anne Arundel County Historical Society

117. In Memory of the Early Parishioners by their Descendants

118. Equitable Trust Bank and Maryland Historical Society

119. Magothy United Methodist Church, Historic Annapolis, Inc., and Maryland Historical Society

120. The Hammons-Harwood Association, Inc.

121. Society of Mareen Duvall Descendants

122. Anne Arundel Chapter, N.S.D.A.R.

123. Shipley's Choice Community Association, Inc., and Maryland Historical Society

124. Eastport Historical Committee and Maryland Historical Trust

125. The Severn Crossroads Foundation, Inc. and the Maryland Historical Society

126. Linthicum Heights Improvement Association, Anne Arundel County Historical Society and the Maryland Historical Society

127. Charles County Civil War Centennial Commission

128. Archbishop Neale Council, Knights of Columbus, No. 2279; Bryantown Council, Knights of Columbus, No. 2293; Saint Thomas Manor General Assembly, Fourth Degree Knights of Columbus

129. Maryland Society, Sons of the American Revolution

130. The National Society of Descendants of Lords of the Maryland Manors

131. Officials of Charles County

132. School Children of Charles County

133. National Society, Colonial Dames of America, of the District of Columbia

134. Charles County Council of Rural Women's Clubs

135. Members of the Bar of Charles County

136. Saint Columbia Lodge No. 150, A.F. & A.M.; La Plata

137. La Plata Volunteer Fire Department

138. The Maryland Realty Investment Trust, Inc.

139. The Episcopal Parishes of Charles County

140. The Society for the Preservation of Maryland Antiquities

141. Pomona Grange of Prince George's County, George Washington Bicentennial

142. Leander McCormick Goodhart

143. George Washington Bicentennial Commission

144. Members and Friends of this Parish, George Washington Bicentennial

145. The Congregation, George Washington Bicentennial

146. The Maryland-National Capital Park and Planning Commission

147. Vestry of St. Thomas Parish, Prince Georges County and Maryland Historical Society

148. "Forest Garden Club", Prince George's County George Washington Bicentennial

149. Prince George's County Historical Society

150. State of Maryland

151. Masonic Lodge, Prince George's County

152. Magruder Chapter, D.C.D.A.R.

153. Church Home and Hospital and the Maryland Historical Society

154. Old Kent Chapter, Daughters of the American Revolution

155. Montgomery County Historical Society and Maryland Civil War Centennial Commission

156. City of Havre de Grace

157. Potomac Electric Power Company, Charles County Garden Club and Maryland Historical Society

158. The Friends of Popular Hill Mansion and the Maryland Historical Society

159. National Star-Spangled Banner Centennial Pilgrimage, September 14, 1914

U.S. NAVAL ACADEMY - COLOR PARADE - "Commissioning Week" each year is marked by a series of events, one of which is the Color Parade. Of the 36 companies of Midshipmen, the company which accumulates the most points for academic, professional and intramural excellence is given the privilege to carry the colors for the brigade for the next year.